Your Debut as an: Elite Thought Leader

Discover the "Secrets" the Most
Successful Thought Leaders Today Use
to Reach Millions of Raving Fans to Change Lives
and Earn a Great Living

The Proven Platform that Will Put You in Front of the People Who Need What You Do

How the leaders who focus on these
4 Pillars dominate their market

Are you a Thought Leader?

You may not typically use those words to describe what you do.

That's ok, we use that term to mean anyone who is working to solve a problem or effect change in their communities or in the world in general...

... people who influence and inspire others to achieve a desired outcome.

Paul B. Thornton gives a great definition in his book, <u>Management Principles and Practices:</u>

> "Thought Leaders harness the power of ideas to actualize change. They stretch their followers by helping them envision new possibilities."

You may align more with the term "Creator", "Niche Blogger", "Influencer", or "Coach" and that's fine too. You'll see all these terms used throughout the book. Regardless of which term you see used, if what you do makes a difference to people, animals, or the planet, the principles in this book can help you do more, faster and on a larger scale.

(Psst! Write in this book!)

Forget the rules about books. This isn't an ordinary book, it's a tool for building your Leader Stage and the key to a successful debut as a thought leader in your niche.

Why do you need a Leader Stage?

Because the world has changed and most of the Gatekeepers are gone. This is a good news / bad news situation. Gatekeepers were the "bouncers" who could lift the velvet rope to allow someone entrance into the elite inner circle. Getting past the Gatekeepers used to be the hardest part of becoming a leader. Now, most of them are gone. Technology has leveled the playing field and we don't need someone to "let us in".

That's the good news.

The bad news is, the gatekeepers were also the promoters. In the old days, people who got past the gatekeepers had it made. Once you were "in", there was a system in place for rocketing you to fame and fortune, all you had to do was show up.

Those days are gone too.

Today, no one has to let you in, but no one is going to promote you either. There is no one on the other side of the velvet rope to choose you.

That means it's all on you. The sad thing is, many people don't realize this shift has taken place. They're still trying to "get discovered". They're standing at the velvet rope anxiously waiting for someone to lift it for them.

No one is coming.

No one ever will.

The only one in charge of promoting your work to the world is you.

The Leader Stage

A stage is a focal point for attention. We have all learned to sit still and pay attention to what's happening on a stage (or in the front of a room). We made up the term "Leader Stage" to use as a metaphor when we talk about attracting (and holding) the attention of your ideal audience.

Your Leader Stage is the way you will do that. It will build an audience of fans who stick with you, fans who buy what you create, who listen to your podcasts, who engage with you on social media, and who will promote you to their friends. Without an audience, you don't have a business, period.

A Leader Stage has a lot of working parts and needs a good deal of thought and creativity in the building process. We've included many of the tools we thought would be most helpful to help you in your brainstorming, planning, and execution. You can get the entire download folder here http://bonus.yourdebuthq.com/

For Serious Business Builders

Occasionally throughout the book you'll see references to Backstage and the Thought Leaders Network. These are service centers we created to help you turbo-charge building your Leader Stage and extending your reach. These services centers are the fast-lane from where you are to where you want to be:

Backstage is where you'll find in-depth training and workshops and done-for-you services. You can have your launches designed, funnels set up, landing pages built, email sequences written, ads managed, and one on one help with anything to do with stage building and maintenance. You can also access Influencer Marketing and create income streams for yourself through the influencer marketplace. Members can both buy and sell sponsored content and display ads. It's where you can earn an income *and* grow your audience. We actively promote the marketplace to brands who want to purchase sponsored content and ads on influencer blogs that reach their target audience. We are always picking up cool tools to share with our Backstage members.

Thought Leaders Network is where people looking for someone in your niche can book you as a speaker or invite you to be interviewed on a show or any number of things that will either pay you directly or promote you to a larger audience. Think of it like a speakers' bureau or a management agency, we help our network members get in front of the right audiences.

The best way to use these service centers is to start with Backstage for the actual building of your Leader Stage, getting your automation tools set up, creating your products, etc.

You can join Backstage here:
http://bit.ly/debutbackstage

Once you have the framework built, the influencer marketplace can help you fill it with fans by leveraging the influence of creators with larger followings. We'll help you find the person who has the ear of your best potential fans. You'll also find training and tools for growing your audience. As your audience grows, you can earn your first income here by selling sponsored content and ads on your blog.

The Thought Leader Network can help you get the gigs that put you on stages and in front of cameras around the world. We promote you to the people who are in a position to hire you. This where the serious growth and influence happens... and happens quickly. Because of that, it's important to have a perfectly-functioning Leader Stage and income streams set up before joining the Network. Without those, you won't be able to make the most of the exposure and you'll lose a lot of growth and income. To make sure this doesn't happen, Network membership is only open to active members of Backstage who meet the readiness criteria.

Build – Backstage

Grow- Influencer MarketPlace

Soar – Thought Leaders Network

*You can't know this right now,
but your ragged, rugged
honesty ~ your crazy,
passionate, naked vulnerability
~ your trusting plunge into the
unknown of life at every turn ~
your journey of love and
healing ~ these change your
world, the world of those
around you, and the world as a
whole. Someday you'll know
how important you are.*

~Jacob Nordby,

Fellow Traveler

Welcome to Second Edition of Your Debut as an Elite Thought Leader

When the first edition of this book was published in 2015 and topped the Amazon Best-seller list in the first week, we were thrilled that our little book was so well-received; especially since we had written it as a guide for our private clients and only published it almost as an afterthought without any market research or testing.

We basked in the stories readers shared with us about how they were using the information in the book to extend their reach. Tracy has a great story about a time when he was leading a seminar and mentioned the book. A man in the audience stood up and pulled a copy of it out of his bag and said he had just signed an $80k contract because of it.

Nothing is more satisfying to authors than to hear stories about how their work has helped someone.

We thought our work was done, so we went back to our primary work, helping emerging leaders become luminaries in communities and specialty niches. It's work we love and that each of us has been doing in one form or another for decades.

A few months after the book was published, we started getting a different kind of feedback. The overall gist of it was that the book was great for people who already had a foundational knowledge of what a Leader Stage was and were at a point in their journey when they needed to scale their business and extend their reach, but it didn't meet the needs of people who were just starting out, and needed to establish themselves. We had left out some very important information, so we sharpened our pencils and went back to the beginning to fill in the gaps.

What you're holding now is the second edition of Your Debut as an Elite Thought Leader, a powerful tool for building the stage you need to reach the people who need you.

While we were reworking the book, we decided to build some places where we can interact more personally with you as well as to keep the information in here current. We created a companion website and Facebook group to go along with the book. You can find them at http://yourdebuthq.com and on Facebook at https://www.facebook.com/YourDebutHQ/

This is where we'll post new tools and information until we update the book again, and –most importantly- it's a place for all of us to come together and support each other. Our goal is to build a community of thought leaders and influencers from around the globe.

We also thought it could be helpful to see real-life applications of the strategies in the book...to "put up or shut up". We challenged ourselves to create a new platform completely from scratch using just the principles we teach in this book and share the entire process in real time. You'll have a front row seat to watch it emerge, and pick up some golden nuggets for growing your own business. For a case study, we started building the Your Debut HQ website and social media profiles when we started this re-write. You can see our progress when you visit.

The focus of this book is creating the piece most often missed by people who are building what we call You, Inc. It's about creating a Leader Stage or a platform that lifts you above the other voices in your niche and makes it easier for the people who support or need what you do to find you.

We've made a few important assumptions about you, the emerging thought leader reading this book. We assume that:

1. You're in this for the long-haul and understand there is no magic formula for overnight success.
2. You have a reasonable budget for purchasing tools and promoting your work. The purely organic, get-famous-for-free path will take more years than most people care to wait (if it happens at all). If your business-building budget is less than $1000 per month (most of that is for ads and other promotions), our best advice is to pick up a temporary job or some freelance work

       or earmark your tax refund to supplement your budget. A cash-starved business doesn't grow.

3. You understand that you are in two businesses: the business that serves your niche and the business of running your business. Your strength is in being an expert at the former, and ours is to be the experts at the latter.

You Inc.

In places throughout the book, we'll mention "You, Inc."; we're referring to businesses which are entirely built around one person, *solopreneurs*. If you are building a You Inc. business, it orbits around what you know, what you teach, what you create to solve a problem or to help others get an outcome they want.

It also means you are doing 99% of the behind-the –scenes work in your business. You Inc. tends to look like this:

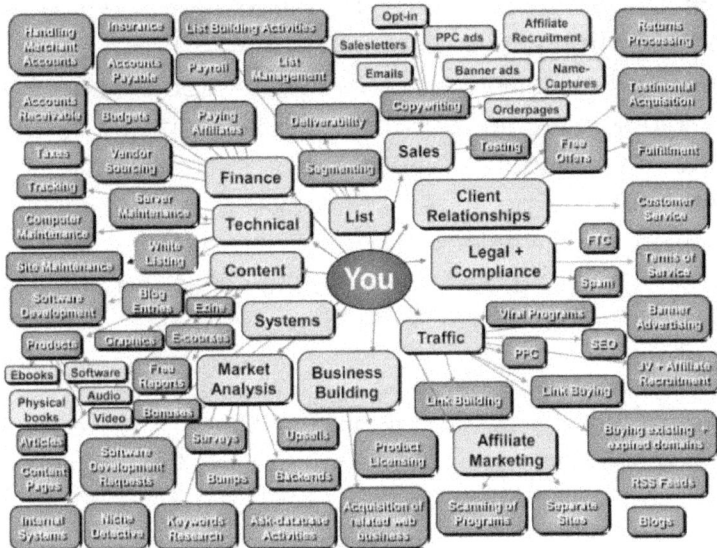

If you've felt overwhelmed by your business, this is why. Most people don't realize how complex You Inc. really is until they see it laid out like this.

Having a properly crafted Leader Stage can manage this complexity and ignite growth well beyond the levels you've likely achieved in the past. It can rocket you into the world of Elite Thought Leaders... the ones on stages in front of thousands of people, the ones helping millions of people achieve the kind of transformation they are desperately seeking. The ones who have created the kind of income that supports them in their work and all their relationships.

How do we know this is true?

Because 95 percent of the clients we have worked with over the years were missing this piece; they had the message but no audience. Most of them had a treasure trove of information they had created about their topic over the years: books, videos, articles, vast amounts of beautiful content that had the potential to help millions of people looking for just that type of solution, but it was locked away on a hard drive hidden deep in a writing cave because they didn't have a vehicle for getting it in front of the people who needed it.

In the case of those who fight for a cause or to grow community programs, they had a world of need in front of them, but few supporters to help them meet that need. They were unable to tap into the vast numbers of people able and willing to help support their work.

In a nutshell, a Leader Stage (or Platform) is marketing and it's what separates the Elite Thought Leaders (the ones known and trusted by millions of people) from the equally brilliant (and sometimes *more* brilliant) unknown expert furiously creating piles of shift-inducing content that no one ever sees.

If the word "marketing" leaves a bad taste in your mouth, you're not alone. Marketing has become associated with hyperbole and disappointment and, as a result, people view it with a jaundiced eye.

In its true meaning, marketing is simply the way two people who want to exchange value are brought together. It's how the world knows to beat a path to the door of the guy who builds a better mousetrap. Without marketing, the brilliant mousetrap inventor must get a day job while mice invade the homes of the world.

The marketing platform or Leader Stage, is built upon four time-tested and proven pillars:

Position

People

Products

Process

Beneath these pillars is a system…as solid as bedrock…that supports the entire structure and ensures that everything *just works*.

we will go into great detail about the Leader Stage as we go along, but the key take away is that it *just works* and it has for a very, very long time.

So unless your situation is completely out of the ordinary (which is possible, but unlikely), **there is a really big opportunity to extend your impact** so you can reach and help more people.

We aren't talking about a short-lived, "sugar-rush" kind of growth; this is the sustainable and responsible kind— the kind that complements your ethical standards and supports your long-term vision for your business.

Skeptical?

We understand. But, as you continue reading, you'll discover that the elements we're talking about aren't gimmicky, revolutionary, or impossible to implement. They don't require you to turn your values upside down or become something you're not.

How to Use this Book

We've designed this book to be an all-inclusive tool to learn what you need to know, put it in action, and create a blueprint for your debut year; the first year on your Leader Stage. To that end, we've included action steps, planning tools, and places to brainstorm.

We've also included coloring pages. At first it may seem a little odd; or, perhaps not, since adult coloring books have become a trend in the past few years. We didn't include the pages to be trendy, though. There's a huge body of research showing that the act of coloring is conducive to focus and creativity. Even university students are using coloring during lectures to keep their minds focused on the material. We invite you to grab some colored pencils or pens and take advantage of the benefits of coloring while you build your Leader Stage.

Keep in mind, you're creating a blueprint for your life's work. When you finish, you'll have a document that you will refer to again and again so take your time and write things out thoroughly. We live in a text and emoji world where we try to communicate as succinctly as possible, and it tends to spill over into all our communications.

Your Debut Headquarters: www.yourdebuthq.com

Get bonus material at http://bonus.yourdebuthq.com

Your Debut as an Elite Thought Leader

This is the time to elaborate on your thoughts. You don't want to look back at an action plan a few months from now and wonder what you meant. There isn't any benefit to hurrying through this process.

Let's get started!

There Have Been Dramatic Changes in the Marketplace

The landscape for those in what has become known as the "Helping Professions" has changed dramatically over the last several years, and will continue to change at an unprecedented pace.

Why? The continued development and distribution of technology has radically changed the way audiences are learning about rising Influencers, how they interact with them, and how they decide where to spend money.

There are three main drivers of this change that are impacting your business. You need to be aware of them and you need to leverage them. Let's briefly run through these game-changers.

1. Search

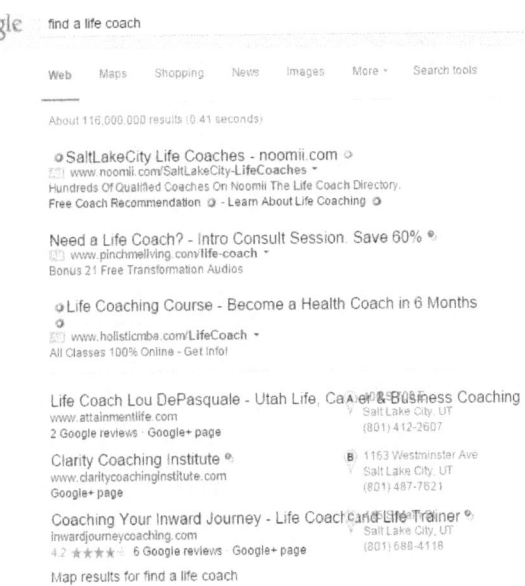

According to Google's data, 97 percent of consumers begin their search for what they want online. The top organic (non-paid) search results get 95 percent of the clicks.

First, a look at the numbers. According to recent poll data from the Pew Internet and American Life Project, **92 percent** of adult Internet users in the U.S. use a search engine (e.g. Google or Bing) to find information online—

with the majority of this group performing keyword searches on a regular basis.

These statistics simply underline what you and we already know:

Search is King.

Everyone who has access to the Internet uses a search engine to find relevant and useful information.

Got visibility?

The upshot of these facts is clear: If you want visibility for your work, you need visibility in the search engines, particularly Google.

Search isn't just king—it's a kingmaker too. High visibility in Google can mean more website traffic, more supporters and referrals, more speaking gigs, and more profit for your business.

For leaders in hyper-competitive markets, search-engine visibility can be the difference between being an unknown also-ran and being the Top Dog.

Getting Google Love

Google has a very simple business model, give people exactly what they want in order to remain the number one search engine in the world so advertisers will continue to spend billions of dollars each year, Google must keep searchers happy by serving up credible, valuable content. It's no surprise, then, that Google promotes sites with good content by showing them first in search results and "slaps" sites with poor content by burying them deep in the results or by not showing them at all. This is called ranking.

Ranking matters

Here's what we know about how people use search engines: after entering a keyword into Google and being presented with pages and pages of blue text links, they generally don't dive very deeply into the results (95.91 percent of all clicks occur on page one).

Additionally, of the page one results, people tend to focus on the top three. According to an Optify study, the top three positions for any given term account for nearly 60 percent (58.5) of the traffic. The top result alone commands an average click-through rate (CTR) of 36.4 percent.

So, it's not enough to be "on Google." If you want to take advantage of the popularity of search, your website needs to be listed at the top of the page or at least above the "scroll line" for the search terms relevant to your business.

2. Social

According to HubSpot, 90 percent of Influencers are on Facebook, and 66 percent of them are spending more time on social media than they did a year ago.

We've all heard enough hype about social media to last a lifetime (or two). But there's a good reason, because there's actually something to the hype.

The social web has truly been a game changer.

Suddenly the norm

The rapid rise of social media has been breathtaking.

Just think: Facebook grew from a curiosity in a Harvard dormitory to a global force with over a billion users ... in less than a decade.

Facebook seems like old news now—a presence in our lives that we take for granted—but it's worth remembering how recently this shift has taken place.

You can love it or hate it, but you can't ignore it. Your audience isn't just *ON* the various social media platforms, it's *GLUED* to them! Just look at these figures from *Digital Insights:*

Facebook:

1.15 *BILLION* users

751 million *MOBILE* users daily

23% of users log in at least 5 times per day

Over two-thirds of users are over the age of 35

Twitter:

Over 500 million users

60% of log ins are from mobile devices

Fastest growing demographic is 55-64 years old

400 million tweets are sent every day

Google+:

Over 500 million users

67% of users are *MALE*

60% of users log in every day

80% of users log in at least once per week

The +1 button is used *5 billion times per day*

LinkedIn:

238 million users

50% of users have a Bachelor's degree or higher

The average LinkedIn user earns $150k per year

Instagram:

The fastest-growing social platform, Instagram currently generates 10 times more interaction than Facebook, 54 times more than Pinterest and 84 times more than Twitter (Brandwatch, 2016)

500 million users every day

5 million photos uploaded *every day*

1000 comments are posted *per second*

Pinterest:

69% of users are *female*

Your Debut Headquarters: www.yourdebuthq.com

Get bonus material at http://bonus.yourdebuthq.com

Top category is food

Most popular brand is Nordstrom with 44 million followers

80% of activity is "repinning"

If that wasn't enough:

YouTube receives over 1 billion *unique* visitors every month

4.2 billion people access social media from mobile devices

Social media generates almost double the leads of trade shows, direct mail, PPC or telemarketing

Around 46% of web users make purchases from social media sites

60% of users say a company's social media presence makes them more likely to refer others

Not just for kids

A common misunderstanding that some professionals have is that Facebook and other networks are just for kids, and thus their target market isn't represented demographically on the site.

But the stats tell another story—the opposite story, in fact.

In the U.S., almost two-thirds of all Facebook users are over the age of 35. Recent Pew research reveals that **two-thirds** of U.S. adults use social networking sites like Facebook and Twitter.

High engagement

As we said earlier, people aren't just ON social networks. They're GLUED to them.

NBC News recently reported the average U.S. Facebook user spends a whopping **135 minutes *per day*** browsing the site.

That's way up from the 15.5 minutes the average American spent just a few years ago!

The upshot of these numbers is straightforward, but we'll spell it out anyway:

Your audience and supporters are on social media sites.

They spend a LOT of time there. They're **sharing, *tweeting, liking, pinning, friending, starring, following, fanning, posting, hash tagging, uploading, retweeting*...** you name it.

People are taking to the web to share their experiences with brands, and what they're sharing with their friends and family members isn't always flattering...

According to a study from the Society for Communications Research, 59 percent of U.S. consumers are using social media to **vent** about customer care frustrations. This isn't just happening on Facebook, but on sites like Angie's List, Yelp, Google+, and others. According to research from Deloitte & Touche, **7 in 10** people who read reviews **share** them with friends, family and colleagues, amplifying the impact of these comments even further.

More and more professionals are beginning to realize that, while they can't control what people say online, they can (and should) monitor and contribute to the conversation in an effort to influence the overall tenor.

They're realizing that having a **consistent online presence** that's focused on **adding value to the customer experience** is the surest way to grow and preserve their reputation—and protect themselves from the stray musings of a few unhappy souls.

Keeping pace with audience expectations

Another big reason to get involved in social media is to **stay relevant**.

Your audience expects it, and if you fall short of their expectations, they'll be more likely to go looking for someone who is more relevant.

Even way back in 2008, a Cone Business study on social media found that **93 percent of donors and supporters expected causes and leaders to have a presence on social channels**, and **85 percent expected them to interact with them on those social channels**.

It's pretty clear that regardless of who your target audience is, you'll find them on one or more of the social media platforms.

3. Mobile

("The really, really big one")

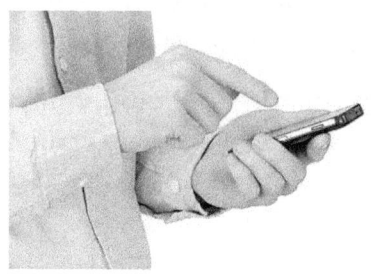

According to research from Mobile Marketer, 70 percent of all mobile searches result in action within one hour!

It's almost impossible to overestimate the impact of the mobile technology revolution.

Look around you: You'll see a steady stream of consumers surfing the web on smartphones, iPads, tablets, and readers.

This is a trend that's hardly slowing.

In fact, the proliferation of cellphones, smartphones, e-readers, and tablet PCs might be one of the most **underestimated** and **under-hyped** shifts in business today.

Your Debut Headquarters: www.yourdebuthq.com

Get bonus material at http://bonus.yourdebuthq.com

As of this writing, 87 percent of Americans have mobile phones. For 73% of them, it's their #1 most-used technology device. Desktop PC use has fallen dramatically with the rise of mobile. Back in 2012 we crossed an important threshold; it was the first time mobile device sales outpaced those of laptop and desktop models and the trend is only increasing.

When you pause to consider what these newfangled devices are capable of, and how quickly they emerged from high-priced novelties to ever-present, "can't live without them"[1] gadgets... it's pretty unbelievable.

Marc Andreessen, co-creator of Netscape, the first widely used web browser, adds some helpful perspective:

> "We have never lived in a time with the opportunity to put a computer in the pocket of 5 billion people."

A recent article in the Economist adds this:

> "The potential of the smartphone age is deceptive. We look around and see more people talking on phones in more places and playing Candy Crush when they're bored. This is just the beginning. In time, business models, infrastructure, legal

---

[1] To illustrate this point, consider this statistic from Unisys: It takes 26 hours for the average person to report a lost wallet. It takes only 68 minutes for them to report a lost phone.

> *environments, and social norms will evolve,*
> *and the world will become a very*
> *different and dramatically more*
> *productive place."*

Search to purchase

Studies show that when people use their smartphones to search for information, they're more apt to take immediate action. They search from where they are and go immediately to what they find.

According to research from *Mobile Marketer*, 70 percent of all mobile searches result in action *within one hour!*

The revolution will be mobilized

It's clear that the future of the web is tied to smartphones and tablets and other mobile devices. More and more, people who visit your website will do so from a small-screened device instead of a hulking desktop or laptop.

What does that mean to you as a rising Influencer?

It means that if you want an effective web presence that supports your goals, you need to have a website that supports a multitude of devices, specifically the smartphone.

A study from Google found that 60% of mobile users will leave a website if it's not optimized for small screens. As a result, Google now penalizes websites that don't offer a good mobile browsing experience with a lower (or non-existent) search ranking. Google rewards sites that provide a great experience for mobile users with higher search rankings.

If your website looks cramped, cluttered or illegible when viewed on a tablet or smartphone, you run the very real risk of turning away your most valuable asset, your audience.

In a weak economy, mobile matters

Think this "mobile" stuff is much ado about nothing? Let's put this into perspective ...

The economic recovery is a sluggish one. People are still worrying about losing their jobs. Millions of homeowners owe more on their mortgage loans than what their homes are worth. Credit-card and student loan debt continues to weigh down U.S. households. The situation is similar all around the world.

These are challenging times for people and they need what you offer more than ever. You don't want to add any additional friction to the process of connecting with you!

A streamlined website for mobile is a new must-have, particularly when you consider that people with smartphones are still turning to search engines to look for information.

What the prominence of these three game-changers means to YOU:

Let's have a show of hands:

How many of you search online before deciding what causes to support or leaders to follow?

How many of you make a decision based on the recommendations you heard from friends on social media?

How many of you carry a smartphone with you at all times?

We all do!

Search, Social and Mobile have changed the way we live, and these trends are only accelerating.

Rate Yourself: Search – Social – Mobile

Is your business Google-able? What do prospective donors or fans find when they search online?

[ ] I dominate the first page for at least 3 search terms

[ ] I'm on page one for my business name

[ ] I'm not on page one at all

ACTION STEPS:

Make a list of your top ten keywords.

Your Debut Headquarters: www.yourdebuthq.com

Get bonus material at http://bonus.yourdebuthq.com

Your Debut as an Elite Thought Leader

When people search for what you do, what words / phrases do they use most often? Include your name and the name of your business (if different) in that list. If your business serves a specific location, add that to the keyword (Dallas horse rescue, Dallas animal shelter, Dallas animal rescue, etc.).

List your keywords here:

1.

2.

3.

4.

5.

6.

7.

8.

9.

10.

Before publishing anything...ever... make sure you've used at least 3 of your top 5 keywords between the title and the first paragraph. If you use one in the title, get the other two into the first paragraph; if you can use two in the title, use at least one more in the first paragraph. Use these 10 keywords consistently.

Keywords are like curry, a little goes a long way. Be careful not to "stuff" your content with keywords. Use them where they fit naturally in the flow of what you're saying.

Be Sure Your Blog Ranks

If you don't have a blog, start one; it's the hub of your business. Create quality content. Search engines, particularly Google, have evolved to the point where they can recognize well-written, authoritative content from poorly written, spun "SEO" articles.

Create and use a content calendar. Search engines reward consistency.

Use keywords as hashtags.

Use keywords for post tags.

Use keywords in blog categories.

Use keywords as YouTube tags.

Register a domain name that uses your top keywords (something like dallashorserescue.com) and redirect it to your main domain name. If you don't have a domain name, see the section about choosing the best one for your business before you purchase one.

How do your social media profiles look? Are you keeping them current?

Are you engaging with fans and followers? Are you providing valuable content?

Are you giving them ways to connect with you right on your page?

[ ] Yes, I'm on top of it!

[ ] Meh...it could be better, my posts are pretty random.

[ ] What Social Media Profiles?

ACTION STEPS:

Pick the best platforms for your business. Keep it manageable, it's hard to be consistent and prolific on a blog and four different social media platforms.

Use the same name across all your platforms. Go to namecheckr.com and put in the name you want to use to see if it's available everywhere you want to be.

Schedule your posts (or use a posting tool with a schedule function) so your posts appear consistently. You'll build your audience faster, and they'll stick around longer when they can count on seeing content from you on a regular basis.

How does your website look and perform on a small screen? What kind of experience are you providing to would-be fans?

[ ] Good user experience

[ ] So-so user experience

[ ] Poor user experience

If your current website / blog doesn't look good on a small screen, switch to a theme / template that does. This isn't negotiable.

Be careful what video uploads you use on your site. Most mobile devices are unable to play Flash (SWF) file types.

Get all the worksheets and action steps here
http://bonus.yourdebuthq.com/

The important thing now is to ask the hard questions and seek out the answers—even if they shake things up a bit:

How do these changes impact the way consumers interact with helping professionals like me?

How do these changes impact my company's growth?

How do these changes impact the way I reach my audience?

These Dramatic Changes Call for…

A Renewed Focus on the Fundamentals!

Given these revolutionary changes we've discussed—search, social and mobile—you might be worried that you are going to have to learn how to use complicated technology or spend huge amounts of time to build your Leader Stage in order to reach your audience.

That's not necessarily the case.

Meet the Four Pillars

Now, let's talk about the four marketing elements or pillars that **need to be optimized to maximize growth** in today's wired, always-on and hyper-competitive marketplace.

The funny thing is, the pillars we're about to present aren't even new!

They're not gimmicks that were cooked up in an ivory tower or by some pie-in-the-sky TED-talk guru.

They're proven concepts that have been tested, re-tested and tested again in the marketplace.

Now, sure, some of the tactics have changed, but the principles themselves haven't.

They are:

Position

People

Product

Process

These are the four foundational pillars *every* business needs to plan for and optimize to maximize its growth potential. These are the pillars that support the Leader Stage which lifts you above everyone else shouting "Me, Too!!!" to your audience.

Data shows, and our experience proves, that **each of these pillars can account for about 25 percent growth on its own, and combined have a compounding effect that can ignite growth to 100 percent or more.**

Your Debut Headquarters: www.yourdebuthq.com

Get bonus material at http://bonus.yourdebuthq.com

Let's run through each element and explore how maximizing these pillars will significantly impact your growth.

Listen to the silent voice of your integrity. When the voice of knowledge becomes the voice of integrity, your emotional body becomes the way it was when you were a child. You return to the truth, to your own sense, you return to love, and you live in your happiness again.

~Don Miguel Ruiz

The First Pillar: Position

Becoming a Trusted Authority

It's a fact: we support people we know, like and trust. A trusted authority is someone who embodies trust and credibility with their audience and supporters.

Becoming a trusted authority is a process, but one well worth the investment of time and money it requires because trusted authorities are not out there in the marketplace yelling "Pick me!" like all the rest.

In fact, trusted authorities don't yell at all, they encourage. They establish trust. They give generously. They don't "hole up" in their website, they're seen in trustworthy places doing trust-building things with trustworthy people.

Persuading or selling becomes unnecessary for trusted authorities because when one of their followers is ready to invest money to achieve a desired outcome, who will they turn to?

They go to their Trusted Authority!

Expert vs Trusted Authority

It may seem like a small distinction, but we use the term "trusted authority" instead of "expert" for a very specific reason.

It's estimated that it takes 10,000 hours of study and practice to become an expert at something. There's no denying that experts know their material. Trouble is, it's common for all that expertise to remain virtually unknown to the majority of people who need it. Being good, or even genius, at something has never been enough. As Calvin Coolidge observed:

"...Nothing is more common than unsuccessful men with talent...unrewarded genius is almost a proverb..."

Experts may have all the credibility in the world, but they often lack a second part of the Trusted Authority formula; Celebrity. Celebrity is an important part of the "trust" factor. The truth is, people trust celebrities. Whether or not all celebrities are worthy of our trust is another issue, but we only have to look at the long history of celebrity endorsements to see the impact. We see a movie star endorsing a certain credit card and we don't stop to wonder what makes that person qualified to make financial recommendations, we just trust and sign up.

We'll talk more about becoming a celebrity in just a minute, but first, let's look at a critical ingredient of the trusted authority formula:

Content

Let's start by clarifying what we mean by "content". Content is everything you create. It includes articles, blog posts, social media posts, videos, courses, infographics, images, etc. It's everything you share with your audience whether you charge for it or not. We'll talk about content in depth in the Products Pillar, but for now, the important thing to know is that *you must have a **quantity** of **valuable content** that reflects your expertise. This content needs to be available in **multiple formats** and **consistently posted everywhere** your prospects are reading, watching, listening, and sharing.*

The important points:

Valuable

Quantity

Multiple formats

Consistently posted

Syndicated (Everywhere)

Valuable - The content you create not only needs to establish your credibility, it *must* provide something your audience values: a handy tip, an answer to a question, a resource or something else that can be used or useful.

Quantity – It's not enough to post one or two well-written articles, your audience needs to see a body of work that demonstrates that you understand their needs. In the Trusted Authority industry, content is like currency, it's what you exchange for the attention of your audience. If you don't have plenty of content, you don't have anything to offer. It sounds intimidating, but there are secrets to creating content that will help you create more in less time. We'll share those with you when we talk about content organizers and frameworks later in the book.

Multiple formats - Everyone has their preferred way of consuming information. Some people are avid readers, others prefer video and still others lean toward audio. Different formats are also better for specific circumstances; a podcast is a practical format for people who want to learn from you as they drive, and videos are easy to watch at the gym. If you create content only in one format, you shut the door on a huge portion of your audience.

Consistently posted- This is an important part of building trust. To be the Trusted Authority, you must be in the "inner circle" of your audience and your content is building a bridge for you to get there. Random, scattered posts here and there make you look flakey and flakey people can't be trusted. When you stick to a schedule, you keep a promise and your audience sits up and takes notice.

Syndicated - This means having your content show up in various places. Your videos show up on YouTube and your social media profiles, your article gets picked up by a dozen media sites and appears as a blog post on your website and a Facebook Note, your book hits Amazon's Top Seller list. When your potential fans see you all around the web, they start to think, "This guy must really know his stuff, he's everywhere!" Syndication is the secret to being everywhere your audience is and a major component of celebrity.

Celebrity shines a spotlight that no one can miss. Just like Credibility, Celebrity can exist on its own and there are plenty of examples of people who are "famous for nothing", we see them on television and in magazines constantly because celebrity tends to beget more celebrity.

Something magical happens when Credibility and Celebrity are combined; it creates a Trusted Authority.

A Trusted Authority is the Go-to person for a specific topic. Dr. Phil is a Trusted Authority, Dave Ramsey is a Trusted Authority, so are Barbara Corcoran, Sir Richard Branson, Tony Robbins, Oprah, and the list goes on and on.

Trusted Authorities are Thought Leaders and Thought Leaders are Trusted Authorities.

The media and the general public want to hear from them, they want to know what the Trusted Authority has to say on a particular topic. Trusted Authorities are *quotable* as well as notable. An important part of your journey to becoming a Trusted Authority in your niche is learning to distill a thought into something quote-worthy.

Claiming your authority and establishing yourself as a leader in your specialty may seem like a daunting task, but don't worry, if you take your time reading this book, take advantage of the downloadable tools and resources, and complete the Action Steps, by the time you are done you will have built the framework for your Leader Stage. Once you have the "frame" or "skeleton" built, it's just a matter of consistently adding detail to flesh it out.

Credibility

When you're the Trusted Authority in your industry, you are above the competition. If you do it correctly, the only thing your competitors can do is vie for second place and fall in line behind you (and we all know that if you aren't the lead dog, the view never changes).

Your audience absolutely **must** see you as an authority they can trust to solve their problem or the champion of a cause they can whole-heartedly support.

Everything from your marketing or outreach materials to your social media posts needs to contribute to your credibility.

There are several ways to help establish your credibility both on and offline.

Of course, the first is to have good reviews and endorsements. If you're just starting out and don't have clients to say good things about you, consider asking former co-workers or someone you helped for free. Anyone with firsthand knowledge of the quality of your work can create an endorsement for you.

Additionally, the tried and true strategy of using paid celebrity endorsements is still an effective one. These days we call it Influencer Marketing.

What is Influencer Marketing?

Influencer marketing sounds new, but it's the second oldest form of marketing, right after Word of Mouth. The earliest recorded example of influencer marketing goes back to 1765. Wedgewood, a manufacturer of china dinnerware, persuaded members of royal families to endorse their products and used the credibility and celebrity those endorsements provided to sell enough dinnerware to become the top-selling brand in their industry. Even today, two and a half centuries years later, Wedgewood china is still a household name.

As the name implies, brands use Influencer Marketing to harness the reach and credibility of a content creator or celebrity (an "Influencer") to promote a product or service to their audience. Thanks to social media, it's not unusual for influencers to have audiences that number in the tens of millions or more. Many of these are raving fans who follow the influencer's posts closely and act immediately if the influencer mentions a brand even casually.

It's easy to see how a sponsored post or "shout out" from the right influencer, who has the collective ear of a particular audience, can spike interest in your content, products, or cause.

Can Influencer Marketing Help You?

Some products and causes lend themselves easily to Influencer Marketing. While it's hard to make a definitive list of what kinds of products and services work best, we can use a broad guideline; if you sell or do something "mentionable", you will probably benefit from Influencer Marketing.

If you provide a quality experience for people, it should be easy to find an influencer in your niche who will promote your work to their audience. If done correctly, it's a win/win situation because these mentions can drive a lot of traffic to your offer and a celebrity's influence is built on providing valuable information, advice or "mentions" to their audience. The more value the audience gets from you, the greater the celebrity's influence...and audience...grows.

Types of Influencer Marketing Content

There are several types of content influencers can create for you depending on your niche and the influencer's specialty.

Tutorial - a video/blog post showing someone how to do something.

DIY Video - Do It Yourself videos are usually more arts and craft style, as in how to tie-dye a shirt, make your own Christmas cards at home; or changing a toilet, building a shed,.... anything that would be categorized as a doing it yourself.

Hauls - video or blog post showing a collection of items, one has purchased. You would purchase a spot in a haul video if you sell a physical item.

Comedic Skits – a scripted video filmed with the intention of being entertaining.

Mentions - the casual mentioning of product/brand/business/person in a video, blog post, or social media post. It's not overtly promotional.

Shout Outs - a tweet/Facebook Post/Instagram post specifically saying your name or brand. It differs from a Mention because it's more deliberate: "Big shout out to____ for ____", where a mention is more casual and is included almost in passing: "I had coffee with a friend at____,and we both loved how adorably they've decorated for the holidays".

Game Play – a video showing someone playing a game and a running commentary about it. Game play videos are most useful for game developers, but if you want to reach a similar audience, you could purchase a mention or a shout-out from a YouTube or Twitch gamer.

Look Book – a look book is like a mini catalog. It can be a video or a series of still images showing an influencer wearing or using a product. There's usually no dialogue.

Vlog – a vlog is a video blog, usually about someone's daily life and appeals to a specific audience. Some vlogs are hugely popular on YouTube and a mention can generate thousands of responses.

Review – this is a video or blog post of an influencer reviewing your product or service.

Native ads - appear in content and look like part of the content. For example, in a travel blog post about Madrid, including a recommendation for a specific hotel and listing its contact information would be a native ad. Native ads are particularly effective because they look like a helpful resource rather than an ad.

Sponsored mailing - is an email sent to an influencer's email list talking about the sponsor's product or service and giving it your personal recommendation. A sponsored mailing includes a link to a shop page or landing page for people to buy or sign up or whatever action the sponsor wants.

Display Ad - is an image or video ad that shows up at the top or in the sidebar of a website.

Finding the Right Influencer

Choosing the right influencer to promote what you do is very important. Someone who has an enormous amount of influence in one niche (audience), may have almost none in another.

Make a short list of those who are influential with your target market. Follow the links to their blogs and social media profiles and evaluate the tone and content of their posts. Does their "voice" match yours or that of your brand? How engaged are their fans? How well would their fans align with what you do? Will they benefit from connecting with you? When you ask another influencer to "share" their audience with you, keep in mind he/she is building a brand too, and their most valuable asset is the relationship they have with their audience, they won't risk backlash by promoting something less than stellar.

Getting the Most from Influencer Marketing

It's important to have a clear goal in mind before contacting an influencer to create a sponsored post for you. Are you trying to grow your email list? Increase your social following? Drive traffic to your content? Register participants for a webinar? Sell a product?

Make the goal measurable. How many sign ups or impressions or sales on your sales page would it take to count this campaign as a success?

When you're thinking about how to incorporate Influencer Marketing into your overall plan for your platform, keep in mind the very short lifespan of a social media post. Website content will be readily available to anyone visiting your site months or even years from now. A social media post, however, is a "flash in the pan", it enjoys a short burst of popularity and perhaps virality, then it's gone, lost in the relentless scrolling of the timeline.

To get the most from your Influencer Marketing dollars, make it part of your larger marketing plan and have a plan for extending the usefulness of the posts. Grab a good screenshot of the post and re-post it on your social media sites and use it as an image on your website and in your marketing materials.

Know the Rules

In the US, all marketing is regulated by the FTC and Influencer Marketing is no different. You can read the regulations on the FTC site, but the short version is that your marketing can't be deceptive or mislead consumers. The concern with Influencer Marketing is that someone reading a shout out or other sponsored material may not realize the influencer received compensation for posting it. In order to comply with the regulations, sponsored material should be identified with "#ad" listed as the first hashtag or "ad" as the first tag so readers can clearly see that the posting was sponsored. The FTC will fine both the influencer and the brand for posts that violate their policy, so it's important to make sure your ad image, text, and hashtags are not deceptive in any way and to ensure that the influencer you choose to work with is familiar with the rules and follows them in all their endorsements.

Influencer endorsements can be costly, but a few well-matched celebrity mentions to the right audience have been known to launch a career faster than any other strategy.

Author, Author!

Next, consider writing a book. This is enormously effective in positioning you as an authority because we are conditioned to see authors as experts. Being the person who "wrote the book" on your area of expertise will pay off for many years to come. The many self-publishing options available today make writing a publishing a book much easier than ever before. Once your book is written, you have something news-worthy to share with media outlets.

If writing an entire book is too much of a task to tackle right now, you could write a chapter or be interviewed for a multi-author book. Tracy knows what multi-author books are in the works and can help you get into one. You can reach out to him in the Backstage group or at TracyAHanes@gmail.com

News Releases

Media exposure will give your business a turbo boost. The hard part is getting it in the first place. The old standby, news releases, are still a great tool, but you'll probably need help getting yours noticed in the crowd.

There's a very fine line between a *press release* and a *news release*. Purists will debate the point to no end, but the gist of it is that a *news release* is something you write and distribute yourself, while a *press release* is sent to a reporter in the hope that the reporter will consider writing a story about it.

How to write a great news release

The format for a news release is similar to that of an article, and written in the third-person. Including a traditional press release header like the one in the example is optional. If you don't want the header, just start with the headline.

FOR IMMEDIATE RELEASE: [Date]

Contact Name

Company Name

Phone # E-Mail

CATCHY HEADLINE HERE (Use a Main Keyword or Two)

Sub headline (optional): Either more detail, or a fascinating teaser to draw them in

City, State: The first paragraph needs to cut right to the chase of the story. Include your 5 W's and H: Who, What, When, Where, Why and How. Make it interesting and include a main keyword again in the paragraph for SEO.

In the second paragraph, it's easy to insert a strong quote. People like to read quotes; their eyes are drawn to them. That's why the second paragraph is the perfect spot. If you can get the reader to read into the second paragraph, there's a decent amount of science that says your readership level won't drop off much after that point. In copywriting, the general rule of thumb is that the only purpose of the headline is to be interesting enough to get the reader to read the subhead... and the only purpose of the subhead is to get the reader to read the first sentence... and so on. You get the point. Every sentence at the beginning of a piece must be interesting.

Use the third paragraph to include a link to your site along with your first soft call to action. Remember not to make it too salesy.

In the fourth paragraph, you can introduce another quote from a different source, and add another link if you have more than one.

Use the fifth paragraph however you like. Perhaps you could talk about the potential long-term consequences of the topic of your piece.

About Your Company: This is a placeholder for a short, 3-4 sentence description of your company along with a call to action link to your homepage.

Once you've completed your news release, you'll need to post it to sites where people will see it. There are services you can pay to do this part for you. The usual charge for syndicating a news release is about $500.00 but may be worth the time saved in doing it yourself.

Want to be featured on a local TV show?

Submit a proposal to be interviewed on the morning or noon show. These shows need content, which means finding people to interview, so they are usually open to proposals as long as they look credible.

How to design a media segment proposal

In general, think of your proposal (the industry term for this is "treatment") as a sales letter... for yourself! Start with a strong headline that stirs curiosity or points out pain.

Here's an example of how someone in the financial niche might do it:

The Best Home Office Tax Deductions Everyone Misses

Then, just like a sales letter, go into who you are and talk about whatever you introduced in the headline:

Best-selling Author, John Brown, Shows Entrepreneurs How to Stop Leaving Money on the Table at Tax Time.

Now create some *talking points*. These are the benefits the viewers will get from the information you'll give. Try to have three to four talking points:

Overlooked Deductions

Little-known Credits

Getting this wrong is like taking a $20 bill out of your wallet every day and throwing it in the trash

Include a mention about any other media appearances, interviews or speaking you've done. If you're working with a media consultant, you'll already have media clips, but if you aren't, you'll have to use whatever experience you may have, "Great TV presence and on-air personality, John Brown has been a guest on XYZ Show". Anything you can include here to reassure them you aren't going to freeze or stammer through the interview will help. That's why first-time media spots are so hard to get; no one wants to risk a bad interview with an amateur. Even links to videos you made for YouTube are helpful.

If you'll be demonstrating anything live, talk about what you'll do and what you'll be bringing in the way of props (don't expect the show to provide anything; if you need a table, have a folding one handy).

Talk about resources you'll offer or anything you can make available for viewers, "John Brown has created a free, downloadable spreadsheet that viewers can use to find their best deductions and start getting ready for the upcoming tax season". If you have a book, state where it can be found.

At the end of the proposal, include all your contact information and all your web properties (they'll want to check you out online). Include at least your website and possibly your LinkedIn profile and of course links to anything that represents you well (don't forget your YouTube channel if it has good content).

If you get a spot, be sure to get a clip to use for future promotions. Once you have your foot in the door, as long as things went well, it's almost like gaining access to the inner circle. Media appearances tend to generate more media appearances.

Back to establishing yourself as authority:

Teach your topic

Just like authors, teachers are seen as experts (and if you want to really hone your knowledge of your subject, teach it).

Don't wait to be invited to speak; you can offer a free seminar in your community through something like Meetup or your Chamber of Commerce (they'll probably want you to be a member before they'll allow you to do this).

Pick a subject your audience will want to know about and design about 30 minutes of content around it. In a one-hour spot, 30 minutes of content allows time for a short introduction, some questions and answers and about five minutes for you to promote your business at the end.

If it's a lengthy subject, break the seminar into parts and create a one-hour introductory one to teach for free. In the Experts industry, these free one-hour spots are called *lead lectures* and they are extremely effective ways of collecting the names and contact information for your audience. The short lecture can be the warm-up for a longer (paid) workshop. In the hour, be sure to give your audience lots of value, you want them to be so wowed by your free seminar, they can't wait to hear what's in the paid one.

So now you have endorsements, you're a published author and speaker, and you're in the media. That's a great start on your Trusted Authority status. Establishing credibility and amassing authority is a stair-step activity with each step leading you upward to the next level.

You should also join professional and industry associations. Just being able to claim membership can be a big credibility boost. Be sure to display any logos or seals your membership gives you on your website and in your marketing materials and mention your membership in your social media bios if you can.

A final thought on Positioning; while optimizing all the pillars is crucial to increasing the profitability of your business, it does very little good to work on any of the others until this one is operating in your favor.

You can pay to reach top-notch potential fans, but it will be useless if you flunk the positioning test.

Start working on your Positioning Pillar right now…and never stop. You can never have too much credibility.

Success is not the key to happiness. Happiness is the key to success. If you love what you are doing, you will be successful.

Albert Schweitzer

The Second Pillar: People

Who's in your audience now, and what are you doing to ensure that more people know about you today than did yesterday?

In the case of Trusted Authorities, we're talking about fans who purchase your books and products, join your mastermind groups, book one-on-one coaching sessions with you, and buy tickets to your events. If you run a community group or cause, we're talking about supporters and donors who show up to your events and write checks to fund your work.

Without someone to buy what you create, all you have is a hobby. As enjoyable as that is, it doesn't reach any of the people who need you, nor does it support you in building the lifestyle you want. Without supporters to fund your work and volunteers to help you carry it out, needs go unmet.

Whatever it is that you do, people are a critical part of your work.

Who's in your audience?
How much do you know about your ideal fans or supporters? How old are they? Where do they live? Are they men or women? Are they married? Do they have children? What kind of jobs do they have? What are they most afraid of? What do they cherish? What do they wish they could do? How do they feel about the

future? What nags at them at night when they can't sleep?

If you don't understand these things and more about your audience, how can you create anything they value?

Additionally, if you don't know what your audience "looks like" you will have a much more difficult time growing it. By this we mean that when you know the interests and demographics of your audience, the strategies we'll talk about later in this chapter to grow it will be less costly and much more effective. When you don't know who's in your audience, you waste a lot of time and money on ads sending uninterested people to your website (we call this driving unqualified traffic) just to have them leave (bounce). This causes your site's *bounce rate* to soar which damages your credibility with the search engines and drives your ad costs even higher.

On the other side, when you can pick your fans "out of a crowd", your ad targeting is laser-focused so you're driving qualified traffic to your site. These are the people who will stick around to read your content, opt-in to your email list, follow you on social media, and buy the products you create.

How do you learn about your audience?

You ask.

In the beginning, you may have to make a few educated guesses. The demographics (vital statistics like age, marital status, education, income, etc.) may be a little hard to pin down, but the psychographics (what they want, like, fear, think etc.) will be easier to guess.

For one thing, they'll be like you used to be.

Notice we didn't say they'll be like you. That's a mistake a lot of leaders make, they assume their audience reflects them.

They may reflect you as you once were. It's important to remember that people are following you because they want something from you. They want an outcome and they believe you can help them get it, so they are like you were before you found that solution. Can you still relate to them?

That depends on whether or not you can still remember the person you were before you knew what you know now. Do you remember what you felt, feared, and wanted before you found what you are offering them?

Does that mean you must have all the answers before you step out as a leader?

No.

It just means you have more answers than they have now. Your journey isn't through either. As you learn more, you can offer more. You're a few step ahead of your audience, but you're all on the same journey.

So put yourself in their shoes and create content from that place. You have to meet people where they are.

Another source of information about your audience is other content they are consuming. What other blogs do they read? What Facebook groups are they in? Use tools like All top and Social Crowdlytics to find what your audience responds to. Read those blogs and join those groups, get to know who else is influencing your audience and what value they offer.

Find the segments in your audience

You don't have an audience of Borg (if you're scratching your head, wondering what Borg are, Google it). Within the main group, there will be subgroups, each with their own demographics and psychographics.

Just as an example, let's assume you're in the natural healing niche. Your audience in general is interested in natural remedies, but the subgroups in there are interested in them for different reasons.

Group A is made up of clean eaters who follow you because they don't want to put chemical cures into their bodies.

Group B is made up of people who distrust big pharma and believe the money-hungry drug companies are deliberately suppressing information about natural alternatives to their expensive drugs.

Group C is made up of doomsday preppers. They believe society is about to come crashing down around us and the only medicine will be what can be found in nature.

Group D is made up of extreme adventure enthusiasts who spend a lot of time away from civilization and want to know about herbal remedies just in case.

You have one big audience with four very different segments. As you can see, something that gets a huge response from one group, may get crickets from the others. To reach the majority of your audience, you must create content specific to each group's needs.

Make Them People

Create personas or avatars for each segment of your audience.

A persona (aka: avatar) is a profile you create that closely represents the people in a group. It's written as if it was for a real person, with a name, age, marital status, income level and so forth. Give the persona fears and desires just like a real person would have. What does your persona want to avoid, what does he/she want to get (or get more of) or avoid?

When you create content with a persona in mind, it's like writing to a friend. In fact, if you know someone who matches one of your audience segments, use their name for that segment's persona, it will make it even easier to create the right content. You know what references to make (will she know what "Borg" are?), and what products to offer. You know which stories to tell and which emotions your stories should stimulate. The people in that segment represented by the persona will feel understood, it will be as if you called each one by name, they'll feel validated, recognized, and will recognize you in turn as a kindred spirit...a Trusted Authority.

When you know *who* is in your audience, it's easier to find the places they hang out on line, it's easier to know what kind of offer they would respond to and to understand what they want you to help them accomplish. Until you know these things, it will be very difficult to convert traffic into fans.

If your personas have very little in common, you may want to segment your email list and send specific content to each list. You can also create products tailored to each one. When you're creating main content that isn't specific to any one segment, send an email to each segment telling them about the content and how it can help them.

Growing Your Audience

When we look at the audience building activities of budding Thought Leaders, we see mostly a scattershot approach.

An ad here and there, a few random social media updates, maybe an occasional YouTube video... with only a vague idea on whether they are getting a positive return on their investment of time and money.

Very rarely do we see coordinated, systematic, and metrics-driven efforts to reach a wider audience and drive qualified traffic to a site.

But this kind of focused, ongoing, and intentional approach is exactly what's necessary to reach more potential fans and supporters in a cost-effective—not to mention satisfying—manner.

A once-in-awhile, ad hoc marketing strategy is not going to get the results leaders need to achieve consistent growth.

No wonder so many leaders struggle to get their message heard or their cause supported:

They're doing it wrong…But don't worry, that won't be you.

We've said it before and we'll say a few more times before the end of this book, without an audience, you don't have a business, regardless of what you do.

In fact, the staggering number of people who earn millions of dollars per year from their audiences on places like YouTube and Twitch, (but sell absolutely nothing) are proof that having an audience is the single most important factor to earning big money online.

There you have it, that's the "secret" to creating the laptop lifestyle.

The people who struggle to earn a living, the ones who will eventually give up and the ones who will join the bitter crowd of you-can't-make-a-living-online critics are the ones who mistakenly believed, "If you build it, they will come".   The truth is closer to, "If you gather them, they will buy".

Take a minute to absorb that. It's a huge shift in thinking and completely opposite to what you might be doing (or planning to do) right now.

Building an audience is so important, we struggled and debated for weeks as to whether or not it should be the first of the Four Pillars. We finally settled on Positon as the first because we assumed most people reading this book already have a good amount of content created that could be used to build credibility and make them "Google-able".

Once you have a few good results showing up in searches for your name, it's time to shift your focus to building your audience.

The Effective Audience Building Mix

Earn an Audience
We talked earlier about "borrowing" an influencer's audience by purchasing sponsored content from them. There are three additional audience-building strategies that let you leverage someone else's audience for free. The key to being successful with any or all of these is in building relationships with the influencers first. This

probably won't happen overnight, so build a short list of 10-20 influencers you want to work with and plan to invest a couple of hours each day analyzing and interacting with their content. You'll also need a longer list of the top 200 or so influencers in your niche. This larger list will be the one you use when you start asking for interviews or links. Getting the attention of an influencer is a numbers game, you'll need a good-sized list for that. If you find someone on your large list to be very responsive and supportive, move them to your short list and develop that relationship.

Guest posting

This is content you create for someone else's blog or website. When you've analyzed an influencer's blog and other content for a month or so, you should have a good feel for what they like to post and what their audience wants to see. Put together a "pitch" email that includes some sample headlines and post ideas. If your pitch is accepted, be sure to allow plenty of time for writing and revisions so you deliver the finished post on time.

Interview Influencers

Conducting and posting interviews with influencers in your niche is a powerful way to build a strong network and grow your audience at the same time.

It's important that your interviews provide value to both the audience and the influencer. There are two great ways of doing this.

The first is to ask the influencer to discuss a specific problem or issue in your niche and offer some ideas about how to solve it. You'll get the best interview if you do some research about the influencer you're pitching and align the topic to one of their passions or pet peeves. If the influencer doesn't have a pet topic to talk about, suggest some. Frequently asked questions are a good place to start looking for an interview topic. If you don't know what the frequently asked questions in your industry are, go to answerthepublic.com to find out.

A second source of interview material is to discuss a cause. The influencer you want to interview may already champion a cause. If so, you have plenty to talk about during your interview, just make sure it's relevant to your target audience. If you need to find a cause to discuss, think about what's important to your (shared) audience, and talk about something related to that. If you share an audience of parents of adolescents, you could talk about anti-bullying programs or how schools could make lunches healthier.

No matter which topic you choose for your interview, be sure to prepare a list of open-ended questions to guide the conversation. Give this list to the person you'll be interviewing at least a week ahead of time. Stick to these questions during the interview except to ask for clarification. It's fine to ad lib a question asking for an example or to clarify something that was just said, but you don't want your guests to feel ambushed by questions they weren't prepared to answer.

The format of your interview will determine the equipment you need. If you aren't "techy", don't get tripped up here, recording and broadcasting content isn't as hard as it once was. For an audio-only recording, you can use something as simple as freeconferencecall.com and do a phone interview. When the call is over, you'll get a recording you can upload as a podcast or to your blog. If the recording needs a little editing or to have background noise removed, take a look at Audacity.com. It's free and very easy to use.

For video recordings, you can use a Google Hangout on Air, Skype or a Zoom call, all of which provide a recorded video. If you have a downloadable video file, you can edit it with the video editor on your computer. You can edit a Google Hangout in the YouTube editor.

When you finish the interview, send your guest a thank-you email with the date you plan to post the interview. On the day it goes live, send another email letting them know it's up, Include the link to it and invite them to share the link with their followers. Most influencers, after taking the time to do an interview, are eager to share it. This will bring new traffic to your site, so be sure to have something valuable and relevant for an opt-in to your list.

The single-interview idea can be modified to what we call the Collected Wisdom post (which you may notice is a scaled-down version of the multi-author book we discussed in the Position Pillar). In this type of post, you ask several influencers one question and compile their answers into a post. There are two ways to do this:

1. Ask each influencer the same question to get a post that provides a variety of perspectives on a single issue.
2. Ask each influencer a different question relating to a specific topic. This creates a post with a broader scope.

You may be able to stimulate some engagement if you ask your followers or subscribers to send in questions they'd like to have answered by an expert. It's a good way to involve your audience and have them looking forward to seeing the completed post.

Regardless of how you choose to do your interview, the end result needs to be carefully proofed and formatted. Never forget that a link from an influencer is the same as an endorsement of your content; make them look brilliant.

Be Link-worthy

Hopefully, you follow the best influencers in your niche; the ones who turn out top-quality content all the time. The ones whose emails you open first because you know they will contain something valuable.

In addition to following this kind of influencer, you need to **be** this kind of influencer. Be the person who turns out content people read first because they know it will be good; the kind other influencers are happy to link to because they trust you to give their audience a good experience.

You should still be reading, analyzing and interacting with the content created by the influencers you put on your list. If you're doing your homework, by now, you have a pretty good idea about the type of content each one prefers to write and share. Keep that in mind when you create yours. As you're writing a blog post, or scripting a video or podcast, think about which influencers on your list might be likely to share it. You want your content to be relevant and useful to your audience, and you want it to be link-worthy for the other people talking to your audience.

There are some kinds of content that gets shared more than others. One of those is the List Post. You see them all time, the *Top Ten This* or *Five Ways to Do That*. List posts can provide a lot of value in a quick read, and that appeals to just about everyone. When you take the time to research and craft a well-written, attractive list post, you shouldn't be shy about reaching out to the influencers on your list and asking them to share it.

While we're on the subject of list posts, consider taking this strategy to the next level by creating a list post about the top influencers in your space. This needs to be done well, but if you were to compile a list of the most influential voices in your niche including a photo, a link to their site, and a paragraph about what (in your opinion) qualifies him or her to be included in your list, then contact each person you included and ask them to share it, who would refuse?

Buy an Audience

As you know, there are three types of traffic, or three ways visitors come to your site:

- Earned
- Owned
- Paid

Guest posting, interviews, and traffic from influencers who have shared links to your content are all *Earned* traffic, you did some kind of work to get those people to your site.

Owned traffic is your current audience. These are people who are already on your list. You can send these people to your site just by emailing them. You already know that your income is relative to the size of your list, the math works out to each name on your list adds about $1 per month to your income. We'll talk more about growing that list as we go through this book.

Paid traffic comes from things like ads and sponsored content, you paid a person or platform to send traffic to your site. We already discussed how to harness the power of sponsored content, now let's talk about ads.

Display Ads-

it's been said that everything old is new again and that's truly the case here. Display ads have been a part of the marketing landscape since the days of the Burma

Shave billboards. When the world went digital, it wasn't very long before the first online display ads began popping up on browsers and it's snowballed from there. Banner ads and pop up ads are ubiquitous now. It got to the point that we began to advise our clients to stay away from display advertising and for good reason: it was extremely costly, poorly targeted, and the results were hard to measure.

However, recent changes to media buying have leveled the playing field where (until now) a small handful of ultra-rich companies have been scooping up customers by the boatload.

The first new tool we like is called a **Boutique ad desk.** Ad desks have been around for decades, they are the "middle men" between buyers and sellers of ad space. This has always been a big-business tool, handling an enormous volume of buying and selling every day. Until recently, small publishers (think "bloggers") and small advertisers had to try to find each other and negotiate a deal. The publisher had to manually install the ad on their site and remember to go back and take it down when the run was finished. It was time consuming work. Boutique ad desks handle all the heavy lifting. Influencers with ad space to sell create "media kits" (ad packages) that list the ad spaces they offer and the terms. Ad buyers can research sites with ad space to sell all in one place to find the ones that reach the audience they want to target. They can upload their ad (called a "creative"), pay for it, and get analytics to show them how it's performing. Publishers only have to insert a small bit of code on their site one time, after that, the ad desk serves ads directly to their site, starting and stopping them automatically. For Backstage members, the influencer marketplace offers a boutique ad desk for people who want to sell (or buy) ad space.

Next, we have **Programmatic Buying**. Programmatic Buying uses big-data aggregators to target your ads with laser-precision so that only your best prospects see your them.

What does that mean? Imagine yourself standing in the middle of a huge stadium filled with tens of thousands of people. You know that in that enormous crowd there are people who want to buy your product, and, because you took the time to learn about your audience, you know those people are all wearing red shirts. It helps that you know who you are looking for, but it's still a pretty daunting task to find them in the crowd. Now, imagine that you had a magic wand that would remove everyone from the stadium, leaving only those who were wearing red shirts; that's what programmatic buying does. It lets you filter your ads so you are only paying for people who meet very specific criteria to see them. Facebook has incorporated programmatic buying into their ads platform with the roll-out of targeting, and the other social media platforms have followed suit. Google Adwords offers it as well.

The third enormous change is **Real Time Bidding** or RTB. Real Time Bidding is an auction process that allows you to put your ad in the best possible place for the best possible price. Do you want to be seen on a major site for your industry? How would your credibility improve if your ad was listed on the Wall Street Journal site or ESPN or another site significant to your audience? You can do that now for a tiny fraction of what it used to cost. With real-time bidding, you're buying "remnant" or unsold ad space. It works a lot like Priceline did when it first launched; there, you bid on unsold hotel rooms and airline seats from some of the biggest names in the business, with RTB, you bid on unsold ad space on major websites. You'll need to work with a professional if you choose to incorporate RTB into your marketing mix as it's only available to agencies. It's not for everyone, but if you'd like to explore it further, we can help you get set up with someone in our Backstage program.

Last, but not least, if you've ever been browsing around online and noticed ads for a site you've visited previously following you from site to site, you've seen the last online ad tool in action. It's called **Retargeting or Remarketing** and it's tremendously powerful. The vast majority of people who come to your site are going to "bounce"; they're going to leave without taking the action you want them to take (signing up for your newsletter, scheduling an appointment, making a purchase, etc.). When this happens, retargeting sends an ad to follow them all around the internet, encouraging them to return to your site and take action.

This multi-touch strategy has been a marketing standby for decades (think about how many times you've received the same piece of advertising in the mail), and now it's proving to be just as effective in the digital world.

It's easy to see why we're so excited about these advances in display advertising. Once the exclusive domain of companies with multi-million-dollar ad budgets, this kind of precision targeting and buying and multi-touch reminders levels the playing field for everyone.

Own an Audience

Build an Email List

Before you go to the time and expense of driving all that wonderful traffic to build your audience, make sure you have a way of collecting it. We're talking about building an email list. Failing to build a list is a huge mistake.

There are dozens of horror stories about people who built enormous followings, only to lose everything because their platform (most often YouTube) shut down their account. Never forget that if you don't own the platform, you are at the mercy of who ever does. Even in cases when the account was restored, the followers were not. If those creators had built an email list, they would have been able to rebuild with just a few emails.

Another important reason for building an email list is for selling sponsored content. If another brand or influencer wants to collaborate with you, they'll want to know the size of your reach, so they'll want to see your Google analytics and your subscriber list.

A third, and equally important reason is that owning a list of people who have "raised their hand" and shown they are interested in what you offer gives you a way to reach out to those people when you create new paid content. If you have a list of people who showed interest in improving their finances, when you create a course that goes in depth about ways people can improve their personal finances, you'll have a list of people you know are interested in learning more about that. The size of your email list is directly linked to the size of your income. As we mentioned earlier, people who purposely grow and cultivate their list earn an average of about $1 per month for each name on it.

The Details of Building Your List

Collecting names and email addresses for your list must be done carefully so you don't run into problems with anti-spam laws. Unlike its offline cousin, direct mail, you can't just rent a list and mail people unexpectedly.

The first thing that has to happen is they **must** opt-in to your list and they must know they are doing so.

You could just put a form on your site that said "opt in to my email list" and a certain number of people would do it. However, you'll get a lot more opt-ins if you offer something they want in exchange for joining your list. We call this *something* a lead magnet. Just like its name implies, a lead magnet attracts your best potential followers to your content. In our earlier example, a lead magnet could be a free checklist called **Top Ten Budget Busters**. When people fill out the form to get your checklist, they are also subscribed to your email list. They can even go onto a special list for people who are interested in personal finance as opposed to people who are interested in retirement funds. This way, when you create a course about personal finance and a second course about retirement funds, you'll know which people to send to which offer.

You need three tools to build an email list:

1. An opt-in form

2. A landing page

3. A place to keep your list

The opt-in form

You've seen these dozens of times and probably filled out a few of them. An opt-in form collects the information you want to know about your new visitor. At a minimum, you need their email address. There is a good argument for keeping your opt-in form very short. You may want to eventually know all kinds of important data, their address, phone number, income level, etc. but this is their first encounter with you. Giving up their email address takes a certain amount of trust and the more you ask, the more invasive you may appear. It feels a lot like proposing marriage on a first date. For now, keep it simple, you can always get more information as the relationship develops.

The Landing Page

A landing page is where someone goes when they click your ad or link to your lead magnet; it's where your opt-in form "lives". It's a web page that doesn't have any other purpose than to get the visitor to fill out the opt-in form.

It's extremely important that your landing page looks "right" to your visitor. The first thing your visitor will ask when they hit your landing page is "where am I?" What they see (fonts, colors, images, etc.) on your landing page needs to look familiar or make sense. If they clicked an image ad to get there, use the same image on your page.

The second question a visitor will ask is, "What can I do here?" If you have navigation buttons or links to other things, there is a real danger they will click away before opting in. The only thing anyone should be able to do on your landing page is opt-in and it should be super-easy. Collect the minimum amount of information, make the "submit" button stand out so they can't miss it. It's also a good practice to tell them what will happen when they fill out the form and click submit: "Just let us know where to send your checklist. Put your best email address in here and click submit, and your checklist will be on its way." After they click, they'll go to a "Success" page. This is a page telling them their information was received. It's also a good place to tell them what the next step is "We want to make sure we got your address right, so click the link telling us it's correct and we'll send your checklist immediately."

Don't make your visitors wonder what's next.

A place to keep your list

There are actually two places you should keep your list:

1. An email provider
2. A spreadsheet saved locally

An email provider is a service that, at a minimum, collects your visitors' email addresses and gives you a way to send email to them. You can usually create your opt-in form through your email service which will give you the HTML code to insert into your site to make your form work.

Outside of your email provider, you should keep a backup copy of your list (updated regularly) in a safe place on a flash drive, an external hard drive or in cloud storage. Never trust something as important as your email list solely to your email provider where it could be lost through a data loss or hacking or having your account closed.

Thoughts about your lead magnet

Your lead magnet can be anything your audience will find valuable. Value is the number one consideration in creating a lead magnet. When someone gets your lead magnet, you want them to think, "Wow, if her free stuff is this good, her paid stuff must be incredible", so don't skimp on the value and don't hold back because you don't want to give up your good stuff in a "freebie". Make your lead magnet something that help your reader reach some kind of success milestone in her journey toward her goal. You should know enough about the people who follow you to know what goal they are hoping you will help them achieve and you should also know what the little goals, the success milestones, are along the way. Create a lead magnet that will give a reader even a small victory, you'll have gone a long way toward creating a raving fan. We all know that raving fans are the best promotion you could have for your business and the best way to grow your audience.

A few last thoughts about your People Pillar:

This pillar is about creating awareness and a desire to engage with you, then pleasantly surprising people when they do.

Rate Yourself:

[ ] Do you know your audience segments?

1.

2.

3.

[ ] Do you have avatars created for each of your audience segments? What are they?

What are you doing to grow your audience?

[ ] Paid ads with retargeting

[ ] Consistent Search Engine Optimization (SEO) with keywords

Do you have a lead magnet to build a continually growing prospect/client email list?

[ ] Yes

[ ] No

[ ] I don't have a list

What are you doing today to make sure more people know about your business tomorrow? List everything:

[ ]

Your Debut as an Elite Thought Leader

[ ]

[ ]

[ ]

[ ]

List some things you could implement

Get all the worksheets and action steps here
http://bonus.yourdebuthq.com/

I truly believe that everything that we do and everyone that we meet is put in our path for a purpose. There are no accidents; we're all teachers - if we're willing to pay attention to the lessons we learn, trust our positive instincts and not be afraid to take risks or wait for some miracle to come knocking at our door.

Marla Gibbs

The Third Pillar: Products

Strange as it may seem, it's very common to meet someone who wants to be a Thought Leader and has a lot of great content, but no way to generate income from it.

There seems to be a belief among thought leaders, creators, influencers, whatever we want to call ourselves, that we should be above selling things.

Most of the people we encounter on this path struggle with this and, to be honest, we've struggled with it ourselves; we sold the first edition of this book for 99cents for over a year.

For some of us, it's very difficult to charge people for what we do. This might be because it's so close to our heart, or because we feel called to serve a higher purpose. We've heard some creators say they don't feel right about making money from their content because they aren't "professionals". When we point out that the definition of being a professional is earning money from what you do, we can almost see the light go on in their mind. Most of these obstacles can be overcome by taking a good, hard look at your beliefs and making some mindset adjustments.

We could probably write a whole book on the subject, but we'll save that for another day. The gist of it is that we all need money to support ourselves, our work, and our families and we need ways to generate that money.

Books don't count

Even the most celebrated Elite Thought Leaders -the gurus at the top of the mountain, so to speak -will tell you, book sales will not support your vision.

A book is a tool that you can leverage for credibility and celebrity in order to position yourself as a trusted authority... a Thought Leader. It's not an income stream...unless it becomes one, which is great. The point we're trying to make is that it can't be counted upon to generate significant revenue and should be seen as a tool to build credibility and help generate traffic. That's why books were discussed as part of the Position Pillar.

The secret to building a sustainable income with You,Inc. is to create multiple streams of income. This means earning smaller amounts from more sources instead of a large amount from one source. Not only is this more achievable, it's a safer strategy. If one source stops producing for whatever reason, you still have income from the others.

One of the best ways to understand the power of multiple streams of income is to see how others are leveraging it; success leaves clues. Gael Breton from Authority Hacker has put together an awesome case study on the 23 top-earning bloggers and how they earn money at http://bit.ly/etlcasestudies. It's a long read, but well worth the time. You'll notice how most of them are using three primary income sources, the same three sources we discuss here.

Information Products

Information products are products that complement what you teach in your books. They provide upgraded content for those people who want a deeper dive into what you teach.

Information products are usually offered in stair-steps of increasing value and cost. In marketing terms, this is called an ascension ladder and you've seen it in action dozens of times, although you may not have noticed it.

Here's an example:

You're browsing Facebook and you click a sponsored post from a trusted authority that says:

"My Free Report Shows How to Do This Great Thing You've Always Wanted to Do, Faster, Cheaper and Easier than Ever"

It's something you've wanted to do and you love the idea of doing it faster, cheaper, and easier, so you click the ad to get the free report. The click takes you to an opt in page where you enter your name and email address to get the report (the free report, by the way, is known as a "lead magnet" and its purpose is to attract you and get you to do what you just did... click the link and give up your contact info so you become a "lead").

Soon after receiving the report (or maybe in the report itself), you'll get an offer to make a small purchase, maybe a short course that gives you more in-depth information or a tool that will help you do what the report talks about. The thing offered is called a Self-liquidating Offer (SLO) and that first purchase is called a Trust Transaction because spending a little bit of money is a trust-builder... now you're an insider, a **customer**.

A little while later, after you've had a good experience with the first purchase, you'll be invited to spend a little more on an even more valuable thing, maybe a membership site where you can get great content about that subject every month or an insiders-only newsletter.

After you buy that, perhaps you'll be invited to join a mastermind group where you can have some kind of special access to the trusted authority and from there, you'll probably receive an offer for some kind of increased access, like a one-on-one coaching program or a small live event.

Each of these purchases moved you deftly up the ascension ladder, hopefully in a way that provided a great experience and converted you into a true fan.

Your fans want to go through the same kind of ascension process with you. They want the opportunity to get the best results you can help them achieve and they are very happy to pay you to do that.

We'll talk about creating information products in just a moment when we talk about content creation.

Put Your Influence to Work

While not usually considered a product, your credibility and influence can be an income source for you.

In the chapter on positioning, we talked about how you could leverage the credibility of another influencer to extend your reach beyond your own audience and build your own credibility. If you've done a good job of that and you now have a decent-sized, engaged following of your own, you have influence that others can leverage.

The most common ways of doing that are:

Sponsored content

Affiliate commissions

Selling ad space on your site

Sponsored Content

Sponsored content varies by platform. It may be an email you send to your subscribers introducing your sponsor and talking about the value of what they offer. It could be a social media "shout out". It could be a mention in one of your YouTube videos. It can be a combination of those things or it could be something completely different. The main idea is that you are introducing your audience to the sponsor via one of your platforms.

The same issues we discussed in the Position Pillar section apply here, only now you're on the other side of them. This is your audience and you've worked diligently to build trust with them. Make sure that any sponsors you choose to work with will be a good fit for them. Make sure what they sell or do is done in an ethical way, that people will get good value for the time or money they invest. Their experience with a sponsor will reflect on you, so you want that reflection to be a good one.

All laws about sponsored content will apply to you as well, so make sure you're familiar with them. If you're in the United States, you can find them at FTC.gov. The gist is to be transparent that what you are posting is a paid endorsement.

Affiliate Commissions

Affiliate sales are very similar to sponsored content and the same rules apply. The difference is that instead of being paid upfront for an endorsement, you receive a commission on sales you generate. You'll be given a link that ties a specific sale to you then you'll be paid for your sales either at specific times or when you've earned a certain dollar amount in commissions.

Affiliate selling can be a shorter route to earning money because there are hundreds of sites that offer affiliate programs and setting up your account and getting your links is usually very quick and easy. Most programs will pay you through PayPal so you'll rarely have to wait for a check to come in.

The best affiliate products or services to sell are those you can be enthusiastic about and that align with your audience. If you're reading a great book, post about it and tell your audience what you love about it then end with your Amazon affiliate link to the book so they can go get it and enjoy it too.

You can often find out if a site offers an affiliate program if you look at the footer of their page. There will usually be a link there. If someone sells something you love and would like to offer to your audience, but doesn't offer an affiliate program, it never hurts to contact them and ask if they'd be interested in partnering with you.

Affiliate commissions are usually paid as a percentage of the sales you make, but those percentages can vary widely. You can usually find out what a site pays its affiliates on their Affiliates page.

Another income stream very similar to affiliate marketing is network marketing. Many influencers have grown their businesses significantly by affiliating themselves with a network marketing company that offers something that aligns with their message and their audience.

Selling Ad Space

Once you have a good amount of consistent traffic to your website / blog, you have an asset that can make money for you if you set it up properly.

The first thing you have to have is data. You absolutely must be able to show your traffic stats to a potential advertiser. The most common way to do this is to have Google Analytics installed on your site. You also need to be able to tell a potential advertiser about your audience. If you took the time to build your audience personas or avatars, you know the demographics of your fans and why they follow you. Advertisers want to make sure you're talking to the same people they want to talk to before they spend money advertising with you.

The next thing you need is a way to connect with people looking to purchase ad space. This can be tricky. To do this yourself, you'll need to create an entirely new marketing plan to reach potential advertisers and let them know you are offering ad space for sale. You'll need to research them so you know who might be interested in speaking to the type of people that make up your audience. Then you'll have to invest time and money into placing ads and bringing them to your sales page. Once they contact you, you also have to have a way to let them know the details about ad sizes, placement and duration, as well as a method for billing and collecting payment. It's a whole business in itself.

The Role of Content

Once you've done all the hard and often costly work of getting a fan, you need that fan to stick with you.

Why?

The cost of acquiring a new audience member can be 10 times higher than the cost of keeping a current one.

Whatever metaphor you want to use... mining your backyard... picking the low hanging fruit... the point is the same:

It makes sense (both financially and from an efficiency standpoint) to fully capitalize on your existing fan base and you need content to do that.

In purely practical terms, the more value you can generate from each fan, the less you must spend on marketing to bring in new fans, which means you can increase your profit margins and/or reinvest the savings into your products and services—in the process making your solutions even more attractive to your fans!

The Worth of a Fan

There's a formula for calculating the Lifetime Value (LTV) of a customer (fan):

$ X Frequency=LTV

(Dollar amount of average transaction) x (number of times average customer will purchase from you) =LTV

So, if a typical fan usually spends $100 per transaction with you and invests in three of your products per year, he's worth $300 per year.   (That's a very simple example, but keep in mind that your ascension ladder is moving him to larger and more frequent purchases.)

Now that you know what each fan is worth, one of the most effective ways of increasing income in your business is to increase that number. Despite having easy access to new and effective tools, most Creators (even the top ones!) are leaving money on the table because they're not maximizing the reselling potential of each fan.

In practice, this can mean increasing the dollar value of each transaction or increasing how often people buy. You do this by offering add-on services or upsells or cross-sells. These days there are many cost effective and track-able ways to bring customers back to your business, but you have to give them something to come back for.

Content Creation Secrets

Before you can create anything, you should know what to create, who you are creating it for, how they are going to be consuming it (reading, watching, listening), and how you want them to feel when they've finished it.

What's Your Passion?

Have you ever read or watched something that was completely dull and lifeless? If it was something important, you probably found a way to struggle through it, but if it wasn't, you probably bailed out of it pretty quickly. Our minds are hard-wired to be engaged. A bored mind will wander. Passion will give your writing vibrancy that will be impossible to miss and will engage the minds of your fans and keep them moving through your content.

Even highly technical content can be engaging if it's presented with passion. One of the great thought leaders in business growth, Lincoln Murphy, comes from the SaaS (software as a service) world. Nothing can be as potentially dry as SaaS, but he injects a passion into his writing that makes it almost impossible to leave his site.

Your audience has more choice about who to follow than ever before. They won't allow anyone to bore them when someone more engaging is just a click away. Even if your topic is potentially dry, let your passion for it shine through.

Content that connects

Which of these do you find more engaging:

There are many benefits to learning to play an instrument. Research has demonstrated a connection between the ability to play an instrument and some of the higher functions of the brain, including socialization. Even those who didn't learn to play an instrument in their youth enjoy better social relationships from learning to do so later in life.

Or this one:

Arthur had just played "The Rosary". The room rang with applause. I decided that this would be a dramatic moment for me to make my debut. To the amazement of all my friends, I strode confidently over to the piano and sat down. "Jack is up to his old tricks," someone chuckled. The crowd laughed. They were all certain I couldn't play a single note. "Can he really play?" I

heard a girl whisper to Arthur. "Heavens no!" Arthur exclaimed, "He's never played a note in all his life, but just you watch him, this is going to be good."

Then I started to play. An intense silence fell on the guests. The laughter died on their lips as if by magic. I played through the first bars of Listz's immortal Liebestraume, I heard gasps of amazement. My friends sat breathless – spellbound.

The first example provides good information, and if we had added a few more facts, it would be a very compelling argument for learning to play an instrument as a way to promote brain health.

The second example doesn't include any facts, it doesn't list any benefits of learning to play an instrument. Would it surprise you to find out it's an excerpt from one of the most successful ads of all time, written by John Caples almost a century ago to sell music lessons...by mail? Even with all our technology today, it's tough to sell music lessons via distance learning, imagine the challenge of trying to sell mail order music lessons in 1927. But Caples did it brilliantly.

Why did this ad perform so well?

He tapped into the power of story and emotion. Instead of peppering us with facts and research findings, he told us a hero's - journey story about a man who impressed and astonished all his friends by learning to play the piano without anyone knowing. We feel what "Jack" felt, we're nervous for him when he sits down at the piano, we hear the things his friends are saying and we're eager to "show them". We feel their astonishment when those first, beautiful notes start to fill the air and we can imagine the shocked silence as the last notes of the piece die away.

Making your audience *feel* something is the surest way to form a deep connection with them and nothing does that better than a compelling story.

John Caples knew what all good content creators know, people buy...or *buy into*...something for emotional reasons. They'll need facts to justify their decision, so be sure to include those too, but the heart makes the decision and then the head backs it up.

Almost any emotion can drive an action, they can be divided into two categories

1. To move away from pain

2. To move toward pleasure

Of the two, the first one is strongest so the emotions that drive us to avoid pain are the strongest:

Fear

Guilt

Anger

Protection

The desire to move toward pleasure triggers emotions like:

Love

Lust

Greed

Laziness

Nostalgia

Vanity

Getting people to connect with your content means you have to reach them at an emotional level.

On a subconscious level, we all know our emotions can be manipulated, so we guard them. We build huge walls around them and lock the gates tightly to make us feel less vulnerable.

Story is the key to that lock and science has proven it. A study at UC Berkeley mapped a woman's brain activity while she re-told an emotional event from her life. As expected, the researchers saw her various emotional centers light up as she told her story, but what they didn't expect was that when they mapped the brain activity of the people listening to her, their brains were responding identically; they were actually feeling what she felt.

Regardless of the topic, when your content reaches people on an emotional level, they engage, they feel something, and they act on that feeling.

Before you create, make sure that what you're creating is valuable...not to you, but to your audience, and that it's engaging and connects on an emotional level. Make sure you're creating it from a place of *giving* not *getting* because your motives will come through to your audience as clear as day.

Your Unique Value Proposition

Do you know your unique value proposition? Your unique value proposition is the combination of your expertise and what you do with it that gives people results in a way that is unlike anyone else out there; it's what makes you unique in your niche. It's the reason someone should be following and listening to you rather than someone else.

If this concept is new to you, don't be worried if it takes some time to come up with your UVP. Pinning down what makes you different can take some time and thought, but it's necessary for understanding and communicating with your audience.

Don't skip this step. If you don't know what unique value you bring and why people should listen to you, how can you expect your audience to know? You must be "shareable"; each of your fans should be able to tell a friend why she follows you and why they should too.

Finding your UVP will take some research. To know what makes you different, you need to know who your competitors are and their UVP.

Your Sweet Spot

Your audience research told you a lot about your fans and how they want to engage with you. Use that information to segment and fine-tune your message. You'll need to do this for each avatar or persona you created for your audience.

Now that you know your UVP, it's time to find your sweet spot. When you operate from your sweet spot, your content will always "land" and your audience will grow organically.

Your sweet spot is the place where: what you love to do, what people will pay you for and, your unique value proposition come together.

Visually, it's a Venn diagram, but you might hear it called a "hedgehog" because the Sweet Spot, where all three circles overlap, looks a little bit like hedgehog.

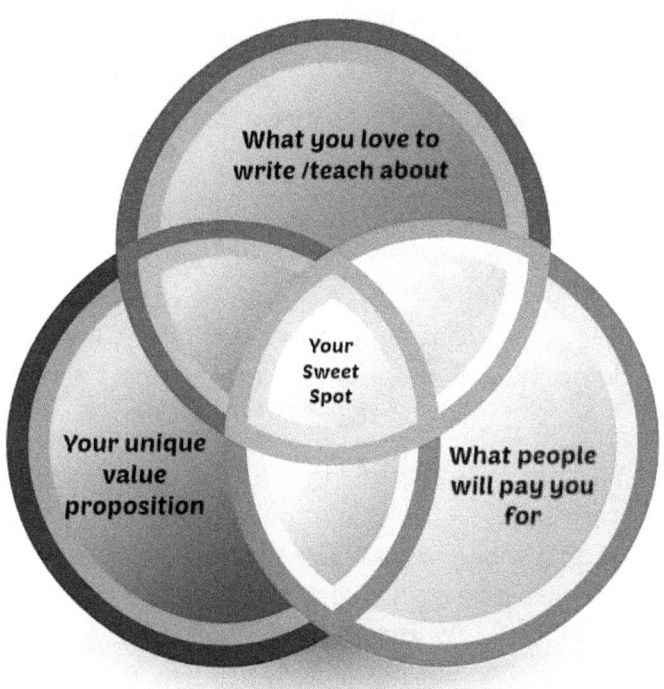

Now it's time to create

There are basically three ways of creating content:

1. Do it yourself

2. Hire someone else to do it (that's called commissioning or outsourcing it)

3. Rework existing content

We'll start with the second one. Commissioning content can be a good idea when you have the budget for it. A little later in this book you'll have a chance to download our Lather Rinse Repeat guide to content creation. In it, you'll find more information about how to get the best results from commissioned content so we won't go into it here.

The remaining two options are for doing it yourself. In third option, reworking existing content, you'll build upon a framework of something you or someone else created previously. There's a famous method created by Brian Dean for doing this called The Skyscraper Method.

In the Skyscraper Method, you are creating derivative content. You start with something that's already good, but could be better. If you aren't the original author, be sure you credit the original author. Start by finding places where you can add value, a resource list, an over-the-shoulder video, create an infographic, etc. The idea is to build on what's already there to make it "higher" than the original.

You can also apply the concepts of the Skyscraper method to PLR content. PLR stands for Private Label Rights. It's similar to ghost-written material in that you can claim authorship yourself and change anything you want. Most raw PLR material won't be very good and will need a significant amount of reworking but it can give you a "jumpstart" when you need it. Make sure to read the license you receive with any PLR products you buy. Some licenses, like a Resale Rights license, only give you the right to re-sell it, not edit or change it; read before you buy.

Now we're left with the nitty-gritty, do it yourself content. All you can do here is roll up your sleeves and start writing but there are a few tools that can make this process a little easier.

The hardest way to create content is to sit down to a blank page and wonder what you should write about. It helps immensely if you have a topic already lined up. When you did your audience research and created your avatars, you found "themes" which reflect the broad interests of your audience; it's why they follow you. Within those themes are topics. Topics are great writing prompts. If "Travel" is your theme, the various modes of travel, destinations, travel preparations, etc. are all topics you can use to create content.

If you plan it right, you can get multiple uses from one piece of content. Rebecca Lieb calls this "Turkey Dinner Content". The "turkey" is a large, well-written content piece, like a comprehensive guide or an in-depth course, you can later "carve" into smaller pieces.

When you plan large content, design it around a broad interest topic in your niche and invest plenty of time into research to make it outstanding. Look at other guides that have been written about the topic, where are the knowledge "gaps" you could fill? If there are comments, read those to look for questions you could answer or information readers don't seem to grasp. Your guide or course should be something that provides a ton of value and something the influencers on your list will be eager to share with their audiences.

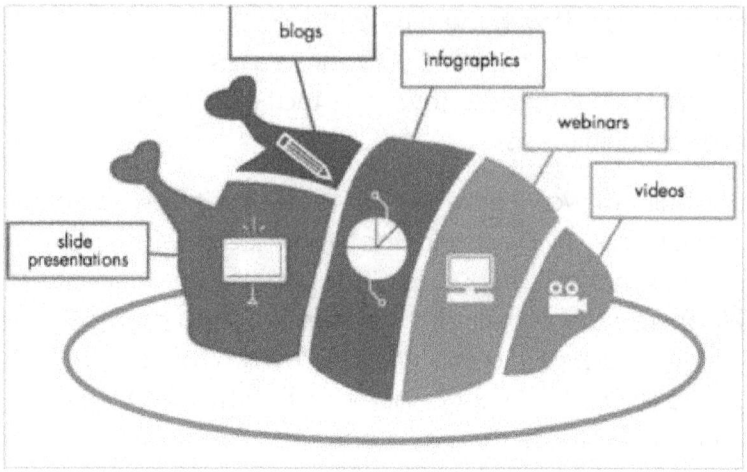

Source: Rebecca Lieb, Altimeter Group

.

Your large content can (and should) provide enough smaller content to fill your editorial calendar for three months. That means you only have to do the hard-work writing four times a year. That makes content planning much easier.

Remember to always create from your sweet spot.

Editorial or Content Calendar
We've borrowed this tool from magazines and it's a great one. No magazine editor sits down at her desk the end of the month and says, "What articles should we put in next issue?" An editor knows what will be in each issue months in advance and has planned accordingly.

We need to do the same thing. With an editorial calendar, you know what you'll be writing about, when you'll be writing it, what form of content it will be and how you'll promote it. If you want to create themed content around holidays or on a timed basis, you'll already have it scheduled.

There's an example of a very simple editorial calendar in the Lather Rinse Repeat Content Guide you can download later in the book if you haven't already.

Content Frameworks

A blinking cursor on a blank page can send the best of us on a downward spiral into writer's block. A Framework can help avoid that.

A framework is essentially a prompt to get you started and to organize what you'll write. It's the skeleton of your work. Some people "flesh it out" completely one section at a time and others do it in passes, adding a little more depth with each draft. Which one you choose is up to you and how you like to work. The Skyscraper method we talked about earlier could be considered a content framework. You can keep it simple and just create an outline that lists the points you want to include. If you're writing a large piece, you can start by writing the Table of Contents then go back and fill in the chapters.

The important thing is to know when it's good enough and stop there. A lot of us fall into the perfection trap and we spend all our time fine tuning a piece when we should be publishing and moving on. One way to avoid the perfection trap is to remember to **create then iterate.** Get a piece to the point that it provides value noticeably greater than the price, it looks good visually (if this isn't your forte, don't hesitate to outsource it. A graphic designer can be working on your cover while you're working on the content), then release it. You can go back and shine it up later and re-release it as an update that original purchasers can download free.

What to Create

One of the questions we hear all the time is, "what products should I create?" The best way to answer this is to look at your audience. If you already have a following with people commenting on your posts, see if there are common questions you could build a product around. Courses that teach people how to do something are very popular. Think about what they want to achieve, if they could snap their fingers and have something happen, what would that *something* be? Create a paid product that gives them that thing.

Take a look at things people don't want to do for themselves and make a Done-For-You product. An enterprising fellow named Bamidele Onibalusi has built a nice business in the freelance-writing niche by creating a directory of sites that pay freelancers for articles. He took the time to do what other writers didn't want to do; research the market and list sites that offer paying gigs to writers. He built an "easy button" for the question, "Where can I sell my writing?". What could you create *for* people who are happy to pay to avoid doing it themselves?

You will find all the material you need to create a successful product in the questions people ask. If you don't have people asking you questions directly, go to sites like Quora.com or Answerthepublic.com and see what people are asking there. We use both sites all the time and have never come away empty-handed. Answer the Public is particularly rich in content ideas.

Don't forget to add the "Should Ask" questions that may not show up online. Those are the questions people "should" ask, but don't because they don't yet know that they don't know. Should ask questions can potentially save people a lot of time or money or prevent them from making "newbie" mistakes.

Why Video Should Be Part of Your Content Strategy

We get it, not everyone is comfortable in front of a camera, but have you noticed the huge upswing in the number of online videos? It's no accident that YouTube is now the second most popular search engine in the world; the number of people who prefer to watch videos rather than read text is growing every day.

If you a little camera-shy, here are some ideas to help you:

1. Remember, it's not about you. Your viewers are paying attention to what you're saying or doing, so take your mind off yourself and focus on the

value you want your viewers to get from watching your video.

2. Script it. Don't read it word for word when you're filming, but if you take the time to write out and practice a script for your video, it will be easier to stay on point and avoid the dreaded "umm" while you think of the next thing to say. Follow the proven formula of speaking:

   a. Tell them what you're going to tell them (Today's video is about_____)

   b. Tell them

   c. Tell them what you told them (The important things we discussed about_____ are this, this, and that)

   d. Give a call to action (If you'd like more information about [topic]you can get my [helpful downloadable resource] on my website at_____)

   Then end the video, don't ramble!

3. Slow down. When we get nervous, we tend to talk really fast. Before you hit the "Record" button, take a deep breath and do a run-through of what you'll say so you speak at a normal pace.

4. Make the camera your friend. Visualizing a friend's face in place of the camera makes it easier to relax and act natural. Talk to your viewers instead of the camera.

5. Do a sound check. Nothing ruins a video like poor sound quality. Before you start, record yourself talking for a minute or so and play it back to make sure your mic is positioned correctly, and you sound great. Watch for things like breath sounds (a filter will fix that), or scratching sounds from your clothes if you're using a lapel mic.
6. Occupy your hands. Touching your hair or face will distract your viewers, so try to keep your hands in your lap or hold something to keep them still.
7. Write out anything your viewers might write down, things like web addresses, shortcodes or email addresses. You can write it on a note card and hold it up or you can add annotations when you edit the video. Note that if you are live streaming, anything you hold up will probably be reversed. The easiest work-around for this is to write it on thin paper (tracing paper is good) with a bold marker and hold it backward (words facing you).
8. Watch your lighting. If you're positioned with your back to a sunny window or lamp, your viewers will only see you in shadow. That's fine if you're in a witness protection program; otherwise, put a light source in front of you. The nicest filming light we've found is called a **ring light**; it's soft and lights your face evenly which is very flattering. You can even get a small ring light to clip on your phone so you look great when you

film or take selfies. You can find both types of ring lights on Amazon.

Facebook's new Facebook Live feature is getting amazing results for people using it. It allows you to stream a live video directly to your Facebook page, group, or personal profile. In a time where Facebook reach seems to be dwindling every day, Facebook Live is helping people extend their reach without paying to do so. Some early testing has shown it increases reach by 1200% or more.

Another advantage of Facebook Live videos is they are interactive. Viewers can post comments or questions that you can answer on air while you're live or in the comment thread after the broadcast ends. The videos can be downloaded and posted to your blog or other social media sites as well.

To use Facebook Live, simply open Facebook on your iPhone or Android (as of this writing, it isn't available on desktop or laptops) and look for the LIVE button at the bottom of the status box. If you'd like to do some rehearsals before broadcasting to everyone, click the dropdown menu that says "Public" and change it to "Only Me". Then you can live stream to your profile and no one will be able to see it but you. It's a good idea to do a few trial runs to get used to starting and stopping the video before you do a public broadcast.

Videos Lead to Higher Search Engine Rankings

Online videos tend to be easily ranked in the search engines if they are optimized correctly. This means your video can come up in a search with keyword related to your business even if your company website doesn't.

Solve for Success

Pop quiz!

Should making your fans happy be the top priority in your business?

NO

We're not telling you to go out there and call people names, but don't bend over backwards to make them happy either. Do you want to know why?

They don't want to be happy...or at least they don't want you to make them happy...they want you to make them successful. They follow you for a reason, they believe you have a solution to a problem they're trying to solve or that you can help them get something they want.

Being happy is great, but regardless of how happy they are with you, if they aren't getting what they from you, they may happily go find someone else to help them. So, when you're creating a product of any kind, always keep their success as the end goal. Make sure you have a clear image of what success looks like for each segment of your audience. Here's how you do that.

Before you create anything else, create a success map for your fans. What is the big thing they are trying to achieve? If you could give each avatar in your audience a magic wand, what would they conjure with it? Now create something to give them a part of that. Everyone wants an "easy button" and they're happy to pay the person who gives them one.

Start with the huge goal at the end then work your way backward to find the little milestones along the way. If their goal is to look great in a bikini next summer, they won't get there all at once; they'll get there in increments and those incremental successes will keep them coming back to you when you build your products around them. The first product may get rid of the first five pounds, the next one may be something that helps them tone up and go down a dress size. Whatever success is for them, baby-step them along the path to achieving it so they can see and celebrate the victories they are having along the way.

Rate Yourself

[ ] Check your beliefs about earning money from your work, are there any that are holding you back? List three reasons why you are justified in receiving payment for what you do.

    1.

2.

3.

[ ] Do you know the LTV of your fans? Multiply the amount of the average sale by the number of times (total) a fan usually purchases from you. If you don't have enough sales data yet to be accurate, use an estimate

$_____/Fan

What is your Unique Value Proposition? State it here and post it near your computer so you stay on course when you write

[ ] Do you have a success map for each of your avatars?

Avatar#1   End Goal

Avatar#2   End Goal

Avatar#3   End Goal

Avatar#4   End Goal

Milestone#1

Your Debut as an Elite Thought Leader

Milestone#2

Milestone#3

Milestone#4

List the ten most frequently asked questions in your niche

1.

2.

3.

4.

5.

6.

7.

8.

9.

10.

List the ten questions people **should** be asking an expert in your field

1.

2.

3.

4.

5.

6.

7.

8.

9.

10.

[ ] Do you have products to sell, either your own or as an affiliate?

[ ] Do you have an ascension ladder in place? What does it look like?

Lead Magnet_____Corresponds to milestone #_____

Self- liquidating Offer_____Corresponds to milestone#_____

Low-end Offer_____Corresponds to milestone#_____

Mid-level
Offer_____Corresponds to
milestone#_____

High-end Offer_____Corresponds to
milestone#_____

[ ] Does your content harness the power of story?

[ ] Have you downloaded and customized your Content Planning Tool and Editorial Calendar?

[ ] List the four large content pieces you'll write in the next 12 months (your "turkey dinner" content)

1.

2.

3.

4.

[ ] Have you scheduled your content for at least the next three months?

Get all the worksheets and action steps here
http://bonus.yourdebuthq.com/

NOTES:

If your actions inspire others to dream more, learn more, do more and become more, you are a leader.

John Quincy Adams

The Fourth Pillar: Process

Positioning, People, Products... those are the three things you must have to support your Leader Stage. The fourth pillar, Process, ties it all together.

Process addresses the "How" of everything: how you establish your credibility and positioning, how you build your audience, how you interact with them, how you create your products and how you release them.

When you have a process, or a system, in place, you don't have to figure out the next step to take. If you have an established process for releasing a new video, for example, you don't have to wonder if you should upload it to YouTube or if you should post it to Facebook.

This part of the discussion can get a little technical, so let's start with a list of terms you may come across as you start planning the processes for your business:

Content – Content is the all-encompassing term for your stuff. It includes any form of written, video, or audio material. It's everything you create in any form for whatever purpose.

User Experience (UX) – UX is everything that happens when someone comes in contact with your business. It starts with how they learn about you and continues throughout their relationship with you and all the points of contact they have with you. The processes you create should all have the goal of improving UX.

Your Debut Headquarters: www.yourdebuthq.com

Get bonus material at http://bonus.yourdebuthq.com

User Interface (UI) – If your fans gain access to you through some kind of technology, the place they do that is called the User Interface. A common example of that would be if you have a members-only website. The website would be the portal (UI). You'll probably only hear this term if you are talking with a web designer or other type of technology provider. The most important thing to keep in mind is that your UI needs to deliver a good User Experience (UX) by being easy to understand and to use.

Funnel – Your funnel, in a nutshell, is your whole process for reaching out to bring in new audience members, converting them into paying clients and keeping them with you as raving fans.

We like to call the processes we develop for our clients "Smart Funnels". We call them that because they adapt to provide a unique experience for each person. This gives each person a better experience with you. If you use a Smart Funnel, you'll know who opened which email, which links they clicked and what they did after that. Instead of having one big list where you send everything to everyone, a smart funnel allows you to segment your list based on actions people take; what they respond to and what they don't. This helps you hold on to the fans you worked so hard to get because you aren't annoying them with things they don't want and you're giving them more of what they do. You're giving them a top-quality user experience.

A Smart Funnel looks like this:

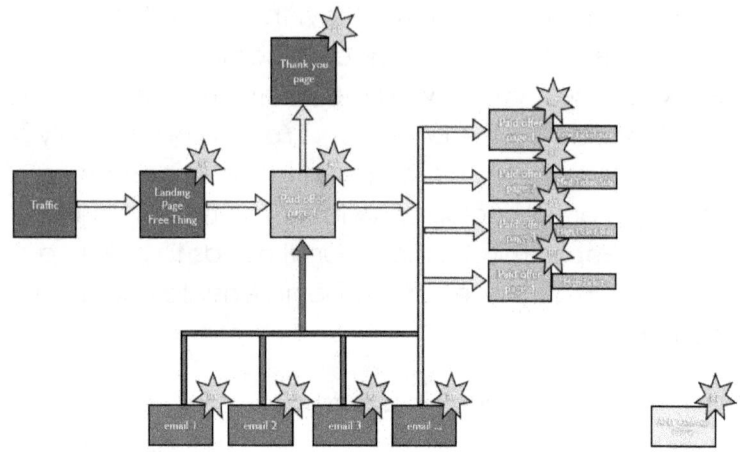

RT=Retargeting point

Traffic – This is just people going to your website or landing page. It's what starts the process and it comes in three types:

1.Earned

2.Owned

3.Paid

Earned Traffic – These are people who find their way to your site through things like Google search or from a press release or article you published. Sometimes organic traffic is also called "earned" traffic because you worked for it, you didn't buy it.

Owned Traffic – These are the people who already have a relationship with you; your list. They are coming to your funnel now because you invited them. It doesn't matter if they came to you originally through paid or organic traffic, they're yours now.

Paid Traffic- These are people who clicked on your paid ad somewhere. It's the most reliable way of sending people to your offer.

Display ad / Banner ad – These are the ads you see usually at the top, bottom, or in the sidebars of a web site. They are very clearly advertisements.

Native Ads – These are very subtle ads that are placed either in or very close to relevant content and look like they are part of the article. For example: just below an article about the top ten family vacation destinations you might see a link that says "Find the Best Family-Friendly Hotels Here." That link will most likely take you to one of the hotel booking sites. It's very relevant to the article so it doesn't look or feel like an ad.

Retargeting – If you've ever looked at an item on Amazon, then clicked away without making a purchase, you probably noticed ads for that item popping up on other sites you visit. This is retargeting. It's a powerful strategy for "nagging" someone who didn't do what you wanted them to do: click a link, watch a video, make a purchase, sign up for an event, etc. In our earlier Smart Funnel diagram, the stars show places where people are being retargeted.

Landing Page – A landing page is where people "land" after clicking one of your links. It could be a page on your website, or better yet, a free-standing page that was designed for a specific purpose. The home page of your site makes a very poor landing page. Whenever someone clicks a link that sends them away from where they were, the first questions they ask when they land on the new site, are: "where am I?" and "what can I do here?". Your landing page needs to answer the first question immediately. Make sure it tells your visitors they are in the right place. You can do this by keeping the colors and images congruent with whatever they clicked to get there and your text should back that up.

As far as the second question, "What can I do here?", give them only two options: opt-in or leave. Don't put any navigation links on your landing page. The only thing they should be able to do on the page is take the action you want: opt-in to your list, sign up for your online seminar, etc.

Opt-in – When someone fills out a form that gives you their name and contact information, so you can send them something (your Lead Magnet), it's called an **opt-in**; they are opting to receive communication from you. It's how they join your list. If you've ever put your name and email address into a web form in order to receive

something in return, you've experienced the opt-in process. Having an opt-in process is a requirement before emailing someone, otherwise, you are spamming them.

It's best to keep your opt-in form as simple and risk-free as possible by not asking for anything more than you need right now, which is usually name and email address. Remember, this person just met you and probably won't feel comfortable giving you a phone number or home address unless they clearly understand why they should (if they were signing up to receive a phone consultation or something in the mail for example).

Opt-in Options:

When it comes to creating opt-ins, you have a lot of options. The most common way is to collect their name and email in a form on a landing page. You have several ways of getting people to your landing page. You can create a QR code they can scan with the reader on their phone which opens a mobile landing page with an opt-in form or you can set up a text opt-in with a keyword. These are both good options when you have people in a physical location, such as at a trade show or live seminar which makes traditional opt-ins harder to accomplish. If you're using video, you can put a clickable annotation (for YouTube) or overlay that takes them to your landing page. A link in a social media ad can deliver people to your landing page and so can the call to action button on your Facebook page.

The most cutting edge (and extremely effective) option right now is the use of chat bots. A chat bot is an automation that engages people in messaging apps like Facebook Messenger. We are currently testing the best ways to use chat bots and sharing our findings with our Backstage members.

Usually, you won't give that many options for joining your list, we just wanted you to see the variety of ways available to you.

It's important to know that text messaging is highly regulated by the FTC and the fines for violations are hefty, to say the least. Automations like chat bots are also regulated by social media platforms and misuse can get your account banned. If you're going to use tools like these, read the regulations. Be sure you are very clear about what you can do and how often.

Lead Magnet – At the most basic level, there are two approaches to marketing: **Push** and **Pull**.

Push Marketing is the classic advertising approach that chases people around yelling "Buy my stuff!" It's often an obnoxious, in-your-face approach and most people don't like it. You'll hear professionals refer to this as "outbound marketing"

Pull Marketing *attracts* the people who are most interested in what you offer. A ***lead magnet*** is the heart of pull marketing and it's just that... a magnet intended to attract the right person (your ideal lead) to you. In industry terms, this is known as "Inbound Marketing" In the previous diagram of the smart funnel, the lead magnet is the "free thing" in the second box.

Lead magnets can be things like a special report, upgraded content, a short video about how to do something, a free consultation, or a trial subscription. Whatever form it takes, the key element is that it provides value *before* you start talking to people about spending money with you. Your lead magnet makes that all-important first impression, so it needs to be well designed and (again) provide something of value.

Upgraded content can be a great lead magnet. A content upgrade is premium content that stems from basic content. It sounds more complicated than it is. The basic content could be a blog post about how a crock pot can make meal times a breeze for busy families. The upgraded content might be a meal planning guide and a recipe book. The content upgrade must be valuable enough to make it worth the opt-in. The nice thing about content upgrades as lead magnets is that they are more likely to be targeted correctly because the person who opts in has already engaged with the related content.

When we design a funnel, we like to create three different lead magnets so we can test them against each other to find the one that generates the most response. This also helps us know if we are on target with our products because the lead magnets we create are taken from our main product and designed to help the reader achieve one small goal. If the main product is built around fitness, for example, one of the lead magnets might be a 7-day meal plan with recipes and a shopping list. We give them what they need to reach the first success milestone in their fitness journey, a week of healthy eating.

You should do something similar. The lead magnet needs to be relevant to their final goal and needs to give them something of tangible value. They need to be able to say, "I accomplished *this* because of (lead magnet)."

Once you have three great, valuable lead magnet "candidates", choose the strongest as the lead magnet for the opt-in and use the other two in the follow-up email series.

Success Page / Thank You Page – This is a page you set to come up automatically after someone does something like opt-in for your lead magnet or make a purchase. This page is important because as soon as your visitor clicked submit on whatever action he just took, a little voice in his head said, "I hope that wasn't a mistake; I don't even know this guy!" The Thank You page, besides being common courtesy, is where you can tell him exactly what will happen next, what he can expect from you. When you deliver according to his expectation, he begins to trust you.

Remember, you're trying to provide a world-class user experience, so don't make people guess at what the next step with you will be.

Self-Liquidating Offer (SLO) – In a funnel, a small purchase step after a lead magnet is called the SLO. The SLO is the first opportunity for a new fan to buy from something from you (and an opportunity for you to recoup some of the cost of getting that new fan). It's an offer for something very inexpensive (usually only a few dollars). It can be used in place of a lead magnet if it's something that has a well-known value. It's a baby-step transaction that helps build trust with you.

In our fitness example, the SLO might be an offer for a work-put DVD for $7. We'd show the offer on the Success page (the page people see after they fill out the opt-in form that tells them what will happen next). An alternative offer could be a free workout DVD if they pay $7 shipping. Free plus shipping offers do very well in some niches.

Do not make the mistake of ending your funnel with your SLO, you're just getting started and if you end with the SLO, you've wasted 99% of your ad spend and abandoned people just as they were warming up to you. Follow up with your new fan through an email sequence.

Email Sequence – Of all the content you write for your funnel, your email sequences will account for the

bulk of it. Just like the name says, this is a series of emails that will be sent out automatically in some kind of sequence. For example, when someone opts in to your list and requests your lead magnet, she should go into a sequence that starts with a welcome email from you that explains what will happen next... how she will get the thing she just requested... and then a series of follow up emails based on whether or not she downloaded or viewed the lead magnet.

Unsubscribe – this is a regulatory requirement and one your autoresponder provider will probably have built in. Every email you send must have a way for people who no longer want to receive email from you to unsubscribe. If someone clicks the unsubscribe link, you *must* remove him from your list and stop emailing him immediately. He may opt in again, later, but until that happens, you can retarget him with your ads, but you can't email him.

Failure Point – These are "weak spots" in your funnel where people can "fall out" by failing to engage. If half of the people who ask to receive your lead magnet never open it, that's a failure point. When people get to your order form but don't finish the purchase, that's a failure point. There are many potential failure points in a funnel.

Contingencies – These are "If / Then" rules you build into the automation of your funnel to overcome the failure points. They work like this: "**If** someone

requests a lead magnet but doesn't download it, **Then** send out this reminder email".

The Bedrock

Your pillars support your platform which supports you, but what's supporting the pillars?

Your Website

It's hard to say enough about how important your website is. This is your "office" and people will form impressions about you based on your site. What impression would you have if you went to someone's real-world office and it was hard to find and when you finally did find it, the exterior was run-down and overgrown with weeds. When you go inside, imagine if it was poorly lit and the furniture was scattered throughout the room without any logical arrangement. Even if the person you came to see was the top expert in his field, you'd probably be put-off by your experience of his office and the impressions you formed from it.

It's the same for your website.

If your visitors have a hard time finding your site, or it looks amateurish, they will have a hard time seeing you as credible.

Does that mean that if you aren't a web designer yourself, you have to break the bank to hire one to build you a gorgeous site?

No.

There are plenty of do-it-yourself web design platforms where you can build a very nice site for just a few dollars. Most of these have WYSIWYG (what you see is what you get) programming that makes designing your site and adding your content no more difficult than creating a Word document.

Take a look at weebly.com, wix.com. Both Weebly and Wix have a free option, but you'll want a paid plan so you can have your own domain name.

There are also done-for-you platforms like Blogger.com and Wordpress (the dot com one, not the dot org one) that are turn-key. Both offer templates so you can choose the look of your site (the theme).

Of the two, we like Blogger for a few reasons. First, Blogger is owned by Google and Google tends to give its own properties a little boost in search engine ranking. We all know how important that can be. Secondly, you can purchase your domain name directly from Google through your Blogger dashboard. This is tremendously helpful because it means you don't have to do any of the technical behind-the-scene work to change your nameservers to point your domain name to your site. If you don't know what any of that means, that's even more reason to go with Blogger. To be fair, you can purchase a domain name through some of the other site building platforms like Weebly, but they charge almost double what Google does. Since the domain name must be renewed annually, the price difference can add up.

If you have already purchased your domain name through a site like GoDaddy or Namecheap, you'll have to redirect it (unless you're using one of their site builders). Most platforms have tutorial videos to walk you through doing this.

While we're on the topic of domain names, let's talk about yours for a minute. If you don't have one yet, give it some thought before you buy. First, make a decision about your long-term strategy for your business. Are you branding yourself or your business? To answer that, you have to look way down the road and decide how you're going to get out of your business. We know it seems strange to be talking about how you're going to get *out* of your business when you're so focused on trying to get *into* it, but failing to have an exit plan has caused a lot of problems for people and we don't want you to be one of them.

If you plan to build up your business and eventually sell it, you'll want to brand it as a business. That means your business needs a name that can also be the domain name. *Pro tip: choose a name that tells people what you do and include a keyword if possible.* Including a keyword in your domain name used to be a ninja SEO technique. Lately, SEO experts are changing direction on this, but we still like it because there are people who, instead of running a search, simply type (what they're looking for).com in the address bar. If your business has keyword-friendly name, you'll get those people to your site. For example, if your business is named Best Herbal Remedies and your domain name is bestherbalremedies.com, someone putting in the search term "best herbal remedies" and adding .com will land directly on your site.

There's a lot of competition for domain names these days, so we recommend finding your domain name first and basing your business name that, rather than the other way around. We also recommend sticking with .com names rather than the other extensions, .net, .info, etc. (unless you run a non-profit or charitable organization, then it should be .org but buy the .com name as well and redirect to your site). The other extensions have more names available, but an entire generation has grown up automatically appending .com to domain names. You'll be sending a lot of traffic to bestherbalremedies.com if you choose bestherbalremedies.net as your domain name.

Getting back to your exit plan. If you plan to eventually have someone succeed you or to shut the business down completely, you might want to brand your business as your own name, Sally Smith, Inc. with the domain name of sallysmith.com. It's not impossible to sell a personally branded business, but the field of interested buyers will be smaller.

When considering a domain name, keep in mind that the most important part of branding is consistency. Before you click "Add to Cart" on a domain name, make sure you can get the same name to create all your social media profiles. We use namecheckrr.com to do this because it will search dozens of social media sites at once and show you the availability for the name you want. It will confuse your followers if you're besthealingremedies.com on your blog, Sally Smith on Facebook, Herbal Healing on Twitter and YourHerbalist on Instagram. It's hard enough to earn and keep your fans, don't make it harder by confusing them.

One last, last thought about names, then we'll move on, we promise. When you think you have a good candidate for a domain and social media user name, take a minute to look closely at how it looks when it's written without spaces (as all domain names and some social media user names are). The folks at Pen Island, Mole Station Nursery, Who Represents, Experts Exchange, and Therapist Finder all wish they had taken that minute.

Essential website pages

Your website doesn't have to be fancy, but it does have to be functional. There are certain pages that are essential for this. The first is your **Home** page. If you're using Blogger, this will be your latest blog post. If you built a Wordpress or other type of site, it's whatever page you set as your first or front page in the menu. Your home page should tell people where they are and what they can do there. Just as if you were sitting at a reception desk, greet them appropriately (in the same tone you use for your content) and help them find what they're looking for by linking to other pages. You might say,

"Welcome to Best Herbal Remedies, we're happy you stopped by. If you're looking for our latest blog post, you can find it HERE (link to post). Our Herbal Healing Master Course is HERE (link to course page) or if you'd like to partner with us, you can learn more about now to do that HERE (link to affiliate program page)."

The next page you'll need is your **Blog** page. Your blog is the heart of your content distribution hub, without it, you are at the mercy of sites beyond your control. A social media platform can disappear almost overnight (does anyone even remember MySpace anymore?), taking all your precious content with it. Your blog will be around as long as you keep your domain name and website fees current. It gives you a place to invite your readers to opt-in for upgraded content and to sell ad space. Your blog needs to look attractive and be kept current with regular posts. Whatever schedule you set for your blog posting, be sure to stick to it.

An **About Me** page is an important way for your visitors to get to know you better. Since your entire business is built around your relationship with your followers, having a place for them to learn about you is essential.

You'll also need a **Store** page to sell your paid products. If you built your site on Wordpress.org, you can use a plug-in called Woo Commerce. If you built your site on Wordpress.com or Blogger, you can use www.ecwid.com to build your store. It's free to use for up to 10 products. You'll need a payment processor for both ECWID and Woo-Commerce. We recommend a combination of PayPal and Stripe because they are easy to set up and are already integrated with WAVE, our favorite bookkeeping tool. There are many other options out there, though, if you need something different.

A **Work with Me** page is how people who want to do business with you can reach out to you to buy ad space, purchase sponsored content, or book you for a speaking gig. If you're registered in the influencer marketplace Backstage, sponsors searching there can message you, but it doesn't hurt to have a page on your site as well.

As a thought leader, you should also have a **Media** page. In the old days, this was called a clip file. A media page is where you post links or screenshots of your media or on-stage appearances. This is where you send people who want to see what you've done or where you've been interviewed in the past before they book an appearance or a speaking gig with you. If "Media" doesn't resonate with your niche, you could title the page "Portfolio" and include links to content you've published on other sites

Most paid ad platforms will require that you have a **Privacy Policy** and a **Terms of Use** page on your site. These don't have to be included in your navigation buttons or menu. Just put a link to them in the footer of your site so people who want to read them can access them.

If you post affiliate links, you'll also need an **Affiliate Disclosure** statement. This can also go into your site footer. Most of them are very simple and to the point:

"Some of the links I post on this site may be affiliate links, meaning that I may receive a small commission if you purchase through my link. It doesn't change the price you pay, and it helps me cover the costs to keep this site up and running for you. Thanks for helping!"

Social Media Profiles

The second bedrock piece is social media. Your social media profiles show up in search results and are part of your web properties. They need to be appropriate for your niche. All your web properties need to have uniform branding, so use the same colors, fonts and cover images across everything. It's a good idea to create a style sheet for your branding that lists the names of your fonts, hex codes for colors and links to images. You'll be surprised how often you'll need this information. When you post an image, use your brand's font for any words you include and don't forget to put your website URL somewhere on it as well. People share images or swipe them for other purposes, if yours are all branded with your website, you may get some viral traffic from it.

There are so many social platforms now, it's hard to know which ones are most effective for you. A lot of choosing the right social media sites to establish a web property depends on your niche. A business blogger would be crazy not to be on LinkedIn, but Pinterest may not be worth the time (or it might be, never judge until you've given it a shot). At the bare minimum, everyone needs Facebook (at least right now) and probably Twitter or Instagram. Pick two or three at most and post like crazy for a few months. You can always branch out to other platforms later.

Social media can be a huge time sink if you get lost in it. Fortunately, there are tools to help leverage your time. You need a tool that will allow you to schedule posts in advance, curate content from other sites, and cross-post to multiple sites. We've listed our favorite in the Automation section.

There's another Facebook tool we really like and recommend called 22Social. It doesn't automate posts, it creates Facebook tabs for your business page, (not your personal profile), that give your page a whole array of functions. At the moment, it's the only tool that makes your tabs responsive, so they can be seen on mobile devices; we already discussed why that's hugely important now. With 22Social, you can build a store (it has PayPal built right into it), host live or recorded webinars, build landing pages, create a paid or free membership program (and handle all the payments through Paypal), and much more. The sales page says it can completely replace a website and that isn't far from the truth. The only reason you wouldn't want to use it in place of a website is the risk that comes with building on properties you don't own. It's definitely a tool worth having. You can see it at http://bit.ly/ydhq22social

Automation

The last bedrock component is automation. Automation allows you to deliver a world class experience for your fans even if you are a "one man show". If you had to personally write every email and manually send your lead magnet to each person who opted in for it, you'd quickly be overwhelmed. People would be waiting a long time for their downloads and you'd never have time to create anything new.

Automation takes care of everything for you. It's like having the world's most attentive concierge working your front desk.

When someone opts in for one of your lead magnets, automation collects their contact information and adds them to your list. It sends them a personal welcome from you, delivers the thing they wanted and follows up with them to make sure they got it. It sends friendly, helpful emails to nurture the relationship and invites them to do more with you. Automation can tell if someone clicked a link you sent in an email (or if they opened the email at all) or if someone watched your video and whether they watched the whole thing or clicked away before it was finished. It learns from and adapts to the way your fans act in your funnel to make sure each person ends up in the right audience segment to have a great experience with you.

Automation tools are critical to your business, that's why we included a complete automation service for Backstage members.

If you aren't a Backstage member, some of the automation tools you'll need are:

Email/List Management Platform- When someone joins your mailing list, you need a way to store and manage their information. There are people who do this with spreadsheets like Excel, but it's much easier to use an email / list management service. These services make it easy to segment your list and manage things like unsubscribes that you would have to do by hand otherwise.

Autoresponders – these send pre-written emails to people at intervals determined by you. If you want everyone who opts into your list to get a welcome email from you, your autoresponder will do that for you.

You can also use an autoresponder to set up *drip campaigns*. Drip campaigns are a series of messages sent to a targeted group to generate some type of action. If you have a list of people who attended a live event last year and you want those people to attend your event again this year, you can set up a drip campaign to go out to them to encourage them to go to your registration site and sign up. A lot of the Email /

List Management platforms like Aweber, Mailchimp, or Constant Contact include an autoresponder service or offer it as an upgrade option.

Digital Delivery Services – Some autoresponders may include this. Most of the files you create will be too large to attach to an email, so digital delivery services store your reports, E-books, videos, etc. and make them available for download by the people who request them. Some popular ones are Amazons3, Box.net, or DPD (getdpd.com) which also offers drop shipping for physical products if you need that.

Social Media Scheduler – This is a very handy tool for scheduling social media posts. With a scheduler, you can queue up enough content for a week, a month, or more to go out to different platforms and schedule them to auto post at specified times. It's really the only way to keep your social media profiles fresh and engaging while staying on top of the rest of your business.

You'll hear a lot about Buffer and Hootsuite, the two most popular social media schedulers, but we like Social Pilot. It combines the best of both Buffer and Hootsuite and lets you connect more profiles and schedule more posts for less than the others. Check it out here: http://bit.ly/socialpilot1

Image Editor- All the latest research is clear, images are more important than ever. You need a way to create compelling images for your blog, social media, products and more. The 800-pound gorilla of image editing is Adobe's Photoshop. If you aren't already a photoshop pro, be warned; it has a steep learning curve. One alternative is to outsource your image editing to someone else. You can find graphic designers on places like fiverr.com or upwork.com. Be sure you get work samples and are very clear about what you want.

You can also use tools like PicMonkey which has a free editing option (although it's worth the $30 yearly fee to become a member to get access to more features and eliminate the ceaseless ads that run on the platform). Canva is another online editor that many people recommend. There are also apps for your phone, so you can edit images and videos without exporting them. We've had good success with iMovie, PicPlayPost, WordSwag, and PSExpress.

These tools will get you started, but it's likely that everyone you talk to will have their own preferences for tools and you may get some great suggestions just by asking.

CRM

A Customer Relationship Manager (CRM) is a power tool for building your business. A CRM is a combination email and autoresponder service with added automation. It stores the usual contact information (think Rolodex) and things like sales history and correspondence. It also takes care of all the automation we discussed earlier. It's the key to building relationships with your fans. People join your audience and become your fans because they believe in what you're doing, they want to be part of it, and they want to have a relationship with you. You want to facilitate that and increase their participation through an ongoing relationship. The CRM gives you the ability to categorize that relationship (fans, clients, event participants, vendors, potential joint venture partners, etc.), and nurture it. Some examples of popular CRMs are Infusionsoft, Salesforce, and Hubspot. Power tools are great time-savers and business-builders, but be prepared for a hefty price tag. Expect to pay a set-up fee in the neighborhood of $2,000 then a few hundred dollars per month based on the size of your list.

Establishing Order

As you can see, your Leader Stage is a complex assortment of components that must work together. Order is your friend, especially if you are building You, Inc. by yourself. Order comes from having processes.

Now that you know each new product or service needs a funnel and each funnel needs a traffic source, a lead magnet, a landing page, an email sequence, and an ascension ladder; you can create a process to get it all done. Once you have a process established, all you have to do is plug in the right content and your funnel will be ready to go to work for you.

You have the tools now to always know what content to create, where to post it and to keep your social media profiles fresh and relevant and your fans engaged, you just need a process for using the tools.

Processes will keep you from spending half your day deciding what needs to be done that day (don't laugh, we have worked with plenty of people who operate just like this!).

If you're a person who likes to make lists, start with that. We're fans of creating mind maps and work flows. Tools like Workflowy and Bubbl.us can help you do this. The important thing to have something written and posted where you can refer to it easily.

Things like Evernote and Pocket can help keep your information organized and at your fingertips.

If you tend to fall into Facebook for hours at a time, StayFocused, a Chrome extension, can help you get back on track.

There is no shortage of tools to help you create and use processes; the trick is to find the ones that you like to use and then use them consistently.

Rate Yourself:

What methods are you using to maximize the three types of traffic:

Organic

[ ] Consistent use of top 10 keywords

[ ] Syndicating content

[ ] Guest posting on blogs with a shared audience

[ ] Cultivating backlinks from credible sites

[ ] Creating high-quality content

[ ] Adhering to posting schedule

[ ] Creating shareable content

[ ] Keeping evergreen content fresh

[ ] Press releases

[ ] Using Facebook Notes

Owned

[ ] Providing real value to email list at least weekly

[ ] 80% value content to 20% promotional content

[ ] Interacting with commenters on posts

[ ] Content aligns with their goals, what's important to them

[ ] Option to join text list

Paid

[ ] Paid social media ads on appropriate platforms

Your Debut Headquarters: www.yourdebuthq.com

Get bonus material at http://bonus.yourdebuthq.com

Your Debut as an Elite Thought Leader

[ ] Using Influencer Marketing to reach new audiences

[ ] Display ads on appropriate blogs

[ ] Native ads

[ ] Retargeting all ads

Website

[ ] Home page is welcoming and helpful

[ ] Has a complete About page

[ ] Blog

    [ ] Attractive

    [ ] Current

    [ ] Posts on schedule

    [ ] Share links on each post

    [ ] Call to Action on each post (inviting to comment, reminding to share, etc.)

[ ] Content upgrade with opt-in

[ ] Has a Work with Me or similar page for people who want to buy sponsored content or ads

[ ] Has a storefront for your paid products

[ ] Has an affiliate disclosure if you post affiliate links

Your Debut as an Elite Thought Leader

[ ] Has a link in the footer to your terms of use and privacy policy

[ ] Has a Media or Portfolio page (or whatever people who want to hire you would expect to see)

Automation

[ ] Have an email service

[ ] Have an autoresponder

[ ] Payment Processor

[ ] Have email sequences written for each funnel

[ ] Have landing pages and opt-in forms set up for audience building and product sales

[ ] Have a digital delivery service set up(Box, DPD, Amazon s3, etc.)

OR

[ ] Backstage membership

Other Tools You'll Need:

[ ] Image Editor (Pic Monkey, Photoshop, Canva, etc.)

[ ] 22 Social http://bit.ly/ydhq22social

For Later:

[ ] Thought Leader Network

Get all the worksheets and action steps here
http://bonus.yourdebuthq.com/

Good, better, best. Never let it rest. 'til your good is better and your better is best.

St. Jerome

Wrapping Up

For this book, we used the metaphor of a Leader Stage with supporting pillars to illustrate what you need as an emerging Influencer, but if you want to look at it another way, you could visualize yourself and your audience on separate islands. In order to reach your audience, you need to build a bridge.

Bridge… Stage… however you choose to visualize it, the bottom line is you need a marketing system in order for your message to reach the people who need you most. These people are most definitely out there, and they are most definitely searching for what you offer; the trick is finding and connecting with them.

It is our hope, that this book has given you some ideas and a framework for doing that.

A Final Thought

As we've traveled this path ourselves, we've found that a lot of people who are building You, Inc. get a lot of benefit from having a tribe… people on the same path who can offer advice, lend a sympathetic ear, and share your journey. If you have a local MeetUp group that you can join, we would encourage you to do that. You're also welcome to join us on Facebook at https://www.facebook.com/YourDebutHQ/

We hope this has been helpful in moving you closer to your goal. If you'd like more personal help, we'd love to

have you join us Backstage, you can do that at
http://bit.ly/debutbackstage.

We look forward to seeing you on the stages of the world!

Lori, Suzanne, and Tracy